PR
MARY BAXTER AND HER MINISTRY

"Mary Baxter truly has an incredible testimony that needs to be shared with all. God surely is using Mary as a soul winner for Jesus Christ."

—*Eldred Thomas*
President, KLTJ–TV, Houston, Texas

"This is one of the most powerful testimonies I have ever read! Mary's descriptions of hell are so real that readers will feel that they are right there with her as Jesus is showing her the horrors of the pit. I wish [her books] could be made available to everyone—to Christians as a warning to continue walking with Jesus, and to non-Christians to show them what is awaiting them if they do not commit their lives to Jesus Christ."

—*R. Russell Bixler*
Founder, Cornerstone TV, Wall, Pennsylvania

"Mary K. Baxter's books have reached around this world and have impacted people in all walks of life. As people get the opportunity to meet her and witness the power of God on her life, they learn it truly is *A Divine Revelation* from God."

—*T. L. Gabbard, Sr.*
Pastor, Wynne, Arkansas

"We have been blessed by Mary Baxter's ministry at our church....Hundreds have been saved and filled with the Holy Spirit, and many have been healed and set free."

—*Winford Walters*
Pastor, Elyria, Ohio

"Mary Baxter has been a great blessing to our church family. Through her preaching abilities, many people have gotten saved and delivered, and a great number of backsliders have rededicated their lives back to God....I believe that her written testimonies will change the lives of countless unbelievers and strengthen the faith of many believers concerning heaven and hell."

—*Jason Alvarez*
Pastor, Orange, New Jersey

"Mary Baxter has preached at our church many times, and lots of people were saved and healed....Her ministry has touched many lives in the kingdom of God."

—*Gladys Boggs*
Pastor's wife, Houston, Texas

MARY K. BAXTER

A DIVINE REVELATION OF THE POWERFUL BLOOD OF JESUS

HEALING FOR YOUR SPIRIT, SOUL, AND BODY

ω

WHITAKER
HOUSE

A Divine Revelation of the Powerful Blood of Jesus:
Healing for Your Spirit, Soul, and Body
(previously published as *The Power of the Blood*)

Mary K. Baxter
marykbaxter1@yahoo.com
marykbaxterinc.com

ISBN: 978-1-64123-270-8
eBook ISBN: 978-1-64123-271-5
Printed in the United States of America
© 2005 by Lowery Ministries International

Whitaker House
1030 Hunt Valley Circle
New Kensington, PA 15068
www.whitakerhouse.com

The Library of Congress has cataloged the original trade paperback edition as follows:
Baxter, Mary K.
 The power of the blood / Mary K. Baxter, with T. L. Lowery.
  p. cm.
  Summary: "Examines the effects of the crucifixion of Jesus Christ in the lives of Christians, as well as the Old Testament practice of blood sacrifices and their relation to Christ's death on the cross"—Provided by publisher.
ISBN-10: 0-88368-989-8 (trade pbk. : alk. paper)
ISBN-13: 978-0-88368-989-9 (trade pbk. : alk. paper) 1. Blood—Religious aspects—Christianity. 2. Blood—Religious aspects—Judaism. 3. Blood in the Bible. 4. Jesus Christ—Crucifixion. 5. Sacrifice—Judaism. I. Lowery, T. L. (Thomas Lanier), 1929– II. Title.
  BR115.B57B39 2005
  232'.4—dc22

                          2004030450

3 4 5 6 7 8 9 10 11 12 13 ʊ 27 26 25 24 23 22 21 20

DEDICATION

This book is lovingly dedicated to the precious
Lamb of God
whose blood was shed to redeem fallen man.
Without the blood, we would be lost for eternity.

CONTENTS

PREFACE

BY
DR. T. L. LOWERY

In Boswell's *Life of Johnson*, Mary Knowles is quoted as saying that Johnson "gets at the substance of a book directly; he tears the heart out of it."

This line describes what Mary K. Baxter and I have attempted in our writing. In four previous books, *A Divine Revelation of Hell*, *A Divine Revelation of Heaven*, *A Divine Revelation of the Spirit Realm*, and *A Divine Revelation of*

Angels, we have desired to "tear the heart out" of our subjects by getting at their essence.

Mary K. Baxter is a choice servant of God, and she is especially gifted and blessed of Him in the realm of special revelations and visions. She ministers as she writes—under a heavy anointing and with a boldness to proclaim the truth. From her eyewitness tour through heaven and hell to special insight into the doctrine of angels, her writing is spellbinding. You always want to read the next page. As her pastor for several years, I have watched Mary grow deeper in the Lord and in her knowledge of His Word. Her use of the Word in her books gives a richness and delight to the reading of them.

Hundreds of thousands of people in many countries have read and been blessed by Mary K. Baxter's works. She is a popular speaker and writer. She enjoys wide acceptance and amazingly positive feedback from her readers.

I am keenly interested in the topic of the blood of Jesus Christ, and I have collaborated with Mary in the writing of this book. We have diligently studied the Word of God, and we present this material with the full assurance that its teachings are backed up by the Bible.

My prayer for this book is that it will be even more widely read and accepted than her other works. May its anointed words speak to the heart of every reader who opens these pages.

My prayer for you is that God will bless you and keep you. May He cause His face to shine on you, and may He bless you in everything you do. May God give you a fresh apostolic anointing and renewed vision as you read these pages. May you be abundantly fruitful in building His kingdom and in reaping the end-time harvest.

PREFACE AND ACKNOWLEDGMENTS

BY MARY K. BAXTER

Why is the blood of Christ important to Christianity? It has been said that "the Bible is a book of blood." It not only gives a faithful account of man's sins and heinous crimes, but also shows God bringing redemption to mankind through the shedding of the blood of His Son.

This book is an overview of what the Bible says about our atonement and deliverance through the blood of Christ, as well as an account of the revelation that God has given me concerning the blood.

The Lord impressed on me the importance of His people knowing *why* we believe in the blood and why it is so crucial to our faith. I have felt the anointing of the Holy Spirit in the writing of these words, and I believe He wants His message to go out. Ultimately, the message of the blood reveals how deeply God loves us and the powerful provision that He has made for us.

I wish to acknowledge a few of the many people who have helped to make this project possible. My pastor, mentor, and spiritual advisor, Dr. T. L. Lowery, has cowritten this book with me. Additionally, he has provided invaluable assistance in the entire project. Without him and his advice, prayer, and help, this book would not have gone forward. I also honor his beautiful wife, Mildred, for her support, encouragement, and valuable assistance in this ministry.

I gratefully recognize and credit those at Whitaker House in New Kensington, Pennsylvania, who have been so instrumental in making these messages from God available to the public.

Most of all, I give grateful tribute and praise to God, who has called me and anointed me to share these messages. I praise, honor, and give glory to God the Father, God the Son, and God the Holy Spirit.

1

THE MEANING OF
THE BLOOD

*"For if when we were enemies we were reconciled
to God through the death of His Son, much more,
having been reconciled, we shall be saved by His life."*
—Romans 5:10

The film *The Passion of the Christ* has received much attention around the world. It has caused hundreds of thousands of people to consider how much Jesus Christ suffered when He bled and died on the cross. Yet many do not fully

UNDERSTANDING THE DEATH
OF JESUS CHRIST AND THE
BLOOD THAT HE SHED IS NOT
FOR CURIOSITY'S SAKE OR
HISTORICAL KNOWLEDGE ALONE.
THE RESULTS OF JESUS'S DEATH
AND RESURRECTION REACH
ACROSS THE CENTURIES AND ARE
AVAILABLE TO US TODAY.

understand the significance of the blood that He shed. They have a general understanding that Jesus died on their behalf, but they don't realize the full implications of this precious gift.

Understanding the death of Jesus Christ and the blood that He shed is not for curiosity's sake or historical knowledge alone. The results of Jesus's death and resurrection reach across the centuries and are available to us today. Many of us have not recognized how Jesus's blood is meant to be applied to all aspects of our lives—how it can bring healing, protection, and deliverance for ourselves and those whom we love. His blood makes available to us greater freedom, power, and deliverance than we can imagine. When we apply the truth of the blood to our lives, we can live in the fullness and power that Jesus provides for us.

THREE DIMENSIONS OF THE BLOOD

One night, as I was speaking at a church in Phoenix, I began to see a vision of the great power of God. The Lord opened my spiritual eyes, and the manifestations of His power seemed to be rolling in on the horizon in a way I had never seen before. I could "see" through the rooftop of the church, and the whole sky was filled with a bloodred mist.

The atmosphere in that church was charged with an energy that I have witnessed only a few times before or since. I saw an angel prompting various people in the congregation and sweeping the carpets in the church, preparing the way for the receiving of the Word of God. I asked the Lord what these things meant—the red mist in the sky and the angel preparing the way. He told me that they were symbolic of the cleansing and sanctifying blood of the Lamb of God.

The Lord also showed me what looked like a big mirror, which suddenly appeared on the wall. It resembled a huge movie screen, and breathtaking scenes began to appear on it. Through it, God began to show me three dimensions of the blood of His Son, the precious Lamb of God, and the sacrifice He made for us at Calvary.

THE HISTORICAL DIMENSION

The first dimension of the blood of the Lamb is a historical one. This dimension refers to the period of time some 2,000 years ago during which Jesus lived on earth and suffered indignities, wounds, and bloodshed. That relatively short space of time is the most significant period ever to have occurred in the history of the world. When Jesus took humanity's sins upon Himself at Calvary—once and for all—mankind was given the ability to be reconciled with its Creator. We were given the gift of being able to draw close to Him in a relationship of love, as He always intended.

THE ETERNAL DIMENSION

Second, the sufferings of Jesus also somehow exist in a timeless dimension. The Bible says that *"Jesus Christ is the same yesterday, today, and forever"* (Hebrews 13:8). God's Word also describes Jesus Christ as *"the Lamb slain from the foundation of the world"* (Revelation 13:8). God preordained Jesus's sufferings in eternity, and they are also considered complete in all of eternity. Jesus's blood is sufficient, and God's mercy is extended to humanity in all of time and space.

THE CONTINUING DIMENSION

Third, there is a continuing dimension of the blood of Christ. The shed blood of Jesus is an ongoing provision for those who have trusted in Him; it still can—and should—be applied in the lives of believers throughout the world.

This provision must remain real to us. One of the things that God said to me in the many revelations He gave me was, "Remember the blood!" We must remember the reason for the shedding of His blood. We are God's redeemed people, and we need to proclaim the One perfect sacrifice of Jesus and His blood, which was shed to cleanse humanity of ignorance and sin.

The ongoing commemoration of Christ's death and shed blood was given to us by Jesus Himself at the last Passover He shared with His disciples. It is a practice that we should neither ignore nor take for granted. The blood of Christ is not to be treated as something ordinary or common. It is precious to God and to us. Without the blood, none of us could have a relationship with our heavenly Father or live in victory over temptation, sin, and the enemy. Through Jesus's blood, we are united with our heavenly Father and given the power to overcome these things.

The continuing dimension of the blood, and what it means for our lives, is the central focus of this book.

THE PROVISION OF THE BLOOD

The blood of Jesus Christ is a crimson fountain that not only flows across centuries and spans the generations, but also supersedes cultures and customs. It breaks down walls that divide people. It can melt the most callous, murderous, vengeful, and spiteful heart known to mankind. It touches broken and despised hearts. It brings hope, cleansing, healing, and deliverance.

By the blood of Jesus, we have these and other wonderful provisions, which we will see throughout this book:

+ We receive the remission (forgiveness) of our sins (Matthew 26:28).

+ We are completely washed of our sins (Revelation 1:5).

+ We are redeemed (Ephesians 1:7; Colossians 1:14).

+ We are justified—regarded as innocent—before God (Romans 5:9).

+ We are brought near to God (Ephesians 2:13).

+ We have peace with God (Colossians 1:20).

+ We are cleansed in our consciences (Hebrews 9:14).

+ We are made holy and set apart for God (Hebrews 13:12).

+ We can have new boldness to approach God and ask for His help (Hebrews 10:19).

+ We can have ongoing cleansing from sin (1 John 1:7).

+ We can overcome the enemy (Revelation 12:11).

A VISION OF THE CRUCIFIXION

Once, when I was diligently praying, I had a vision of the day that Christ was crucified. It broke my heart. I saw the Roman soldiers nailing His hands to the cross using huge nails. I saw His blood dripping and running down. I remember seeing the blood coming not only from His hands, but also from all over His body. He had been beaten so badly that I wanted to comfort Him and do something to help Him.

The men who were doing this terrible deed were cursing and blaspheming Him. Then, the Lord's eyes looked straight at the men, and they fell backward. After a little while, however, they continued to prepare Him for crucifixion. I saw them lift up the Lord on the cross. It was so horrible and sad! I was weeping as I saw this mighty vision.

Then I saw what looked like thousands of angels. They seemed to be invisible to those who were at the crucifixion, but I could see them clearly. The angels placed every drop of blood that Jesus shed in vessels they held in their hands, and then they carried the blood of Jesus to heaven.

The angels were crying as they carried the drops of blood. The precious treasure they carried represented a tremendous sacrifice for Jesus. As I watched in awe, I began to cry so hard that I could not see the vision anymore. I was overwhelmed by the awesome price that He paid for you and me.

God began to speak to me about writing a book on the blood of the Lamb. He showed me things in the Spirit that demonstrated what the Word says about the power of the blood. He began to show me what it means to be cleansed, kept, and set free by this precious blood that Jesus shed on Calvary.

My soul burned within me as the Lord led me to write and talk to others about the precious blood of the Lamb of God. Through various visions and revelations, I began to see, more and more, the absolute *necessity* for the shedding of the blood of Christ. One of the chief reasons for this necessity is that our lives had to be ransomed, and *"the life...is in the blood"*

(Leviticus 17:11). We will look at the nature of this lifeblood in the next chapter.

2

THE LIFE IS IN THE BLOOD

"For the life of the flesh is in the blood."
—Leviticus 17:11

The blood that courses through our veins is a common denominator for all humanity. It is through blood that every human being has physical life. In 1628, physician and anatomist Dr. William Harvey published *On the Circulation of the Blood,* in which he proposed that life is in the blood. The discovery of how blood circulates was perhaps the most significant medical breakthrough of the seventeenth century. This knowledge was essential for understanding how the human body functions, as well as the healing of disease.

Yet the crucial fact that the life of the entire body is derived from its blood was already clearly stated in the Bible thousands of years earlier. God told the Old Testament patriarch Noah,

> *Every moving thing that lives shall be food for you. I have given you all things, even as the green herbs. But you shall not eat flesh **with its life, that is, its blood**. Surely for your lifeblood I will demand a reckoning; from the hand of every beast I will require it, and from the hand of man. From the hand of every man's brother I will require the life of man. Whoever sheds man's blood, by man his blood shall be shed; for in the image of God He made man.*
>
> (Genesis 9:3–6, emphasis added)

THE NATURE AND FUNCTION OF BLOOD

The various compounds and chemicals that make up the physiology of blood operate in a way that is still not fully understood, even with our modern medical advances. Human blood and its functioning in the body is a subject so complex

that an entire medical specialty—hematology—is dedicated
to its study.

This mysterious fluid circulates around the entire body
approximately every twenty-three seconds. It is constantly
in motion, circulating in the heart, arteries, capillaries, and
veins.

> Life, that mysterious something which scientists
> [with their test tubes and modern instruments]
> have never yet been able to define or fathom, is said
> by God to be in the blood of the flesh, so that there
> can be no life without the blood.
>
> ...In the human body there are many different
> kinds of tissues. We define them as muscle, nerve,
> fat, gland, bone, connective tissues, etc. All these
> tissues have one thing in common: they are fixed
> cells, microscopically small and having a specific
> and limited function. Unlike these fixed tissues,
> the blood is fluid and mobile, that is, it is not lim-
> ited to one part of the body but is free to move
> throughout the entire body and supply the fixed
> cells with nourishment and carry off the waste
> products.[1]

The average adult has ten pints of blood in his body.
Normally, seven percent of the body's weight is blood.[2] Blood

is produced in the bone marrow, and it recycles and cleanses itself hundreds of times a day. It circulates through the body, pumped by the heart and oxygenated by the lungs. It delivers nutrients and oxygen, as well as hormones and other substances, to the cells and takes away carbon dioxide and other waste products. Disease-fighting agents in the blood attack and destroy invading germs.

Blood, therefore, gives us strength. It makes growth possible. It is the protector of the body. It fights illness and disease. It is the body's frontline defense against germs, bacteria, and harmful microorganisms. It provides an organized resistance against anything that is harmful to the body. It plays a vital role in our immune system and in maintaining a relatively constant body temperature. It is a harbinger of health and well-being.

A donation of healthy blood is a tremendous blessing to the sick. Approximately thirty-two thousand pints of blood are used in the United States every day of the year.[3] The Red Cross says that an American needs a blood transfusion for medical treatment every two seconds.[4] Blood transfusions are needed for surgeries, the treatment of accident victims, and for people with circulatory problems. Good health is not possible with poor blood, and blood transfusions save literally thousands of lives each year.

BLOOD IS A "RIVER OF LIFE"

Blood is a miracle fluid that only God could make. Though science still doesn't fully understand how blood functions, it is clear that, without blood, life ends. For example, in general, when a muscle stops working, the rest of the body continues working; but if the blood fails, the entire body dies. Blood contains that indefinable ingredient that gives life to every cell in the body.

The Bible reveals the importance of this vital "river of life" that flows in our bodies. God has assigned to blood a certain sacredness that is mysteriously connected to life by His own decree:

> *This shall be a perpetual statute throughout your generations in all your dwellings: you shall eat neither fat nor blood.* (Leviticus 3:17)

> *Only be sure that you do not eat the blood, for the blood is the life; you may not eat the life with the meat. You shall not eat it; you shall pour it on the earth like water. You shall not eat it, that it may go well with you and your children after you, when you do what is right in the sight of the* LORD. (Deuteronomy 12:23–25)

THE CORRUPTION OF THE BLOOD OF MANKIND

Blood is precious and vital to life, but the blood we have today is not the same blood that God originally gave humanity. When mankind rebelled against God, its very nature became corrupt and its blood became tainted. H. A. Maxwell Whyte explained,

> Adam's sin…brought sin and sickness into human blood. If Adam had not sinned, he would not have died. But by his sin, he introduced death into the human family. The human body, therefore, became subject to corruption and decay, and death ultimately comes to each one of us.[5]

M. R. DeHaan, author of *The Chemistry of the Blood*, agreed:

> Since the LIFE is in the blood, according to the Scriptures, and the wages of sin is death, sin affected the blood of Adam and caused him to die. Because [all men are descended from Adam and] the blood of all men partakes of the sin of Adam, it can only be cleansed by the application of sinless blood, *for it is the blood that maketh an atonement for the soul.*[6]

THE FIRST SHEDDING OF BLOOD

We often think that the initial shedding of blood in the Bible happened when Cain killed his brother, Abel. Yet there was an instance before that, and it reveals the necessity of blood sacrifice to atone for sin and bloodshed.

The first occurrence of the shedding of blood was in the garden of Eden when God sacrificed an animal or animals to provide a covering for humanity's shame. When Adam and Eve rebelled against God and tried to live without Him, the Bible says, *"Then the eyes of both of them were opened, and they knew that they were naked; and they sewed fig leaves together and made themselves coverings"* (Genesis 3:7). The fig leaves were apparently not a sufficient covering, for the Bible says, *"Also for Adam and his wife the* LORD *God made tunics of skin, and clothed them"* (v. 21).

Where did these skins come from? Animals must have had to be killed so that their skins could become coverings for the nakedness of Adam and Eve. This shedding of blood was not only for the purpose of covering their physical nakedness, but it was also a covering for their spiritual nakedness. Fig leaves might have been enough to cover physical nakedness, but they would not suffice to atone for sin or enable a person to have a restored relationship with a holy God.

In Genesis 4:3–5, when Adam and Eve's sons, Cain and Abel, brought their offerings to the Lord, we see that the sacrifice of animals to the Lord was acceptable to Him while the offering of crops was not. This was not because tending sheep was a more honorable vocation than tilling the ground. Both were legitimate occupations. For Cain and Abel to be acceptable before the Lord, however, their sins needed to be addressed, and their sins could be covered only through a blood sacrifice. The book of Hebrews says, *"By faith Abel offered to God a more excellent sacrifice than Cain, through which he obtained witness that he was righteous, God testifying of his gifts"* (Hebrews 11:4). In unmistakable language, the Bible declares, *"Without shedding of blood there is no remission* [of sin]" (Hebrews 9:22).

From the time of the rebellion of Adam and Eve, therefore, sacrifices of animals had to be made to atone for the sins of mankind so that they could have a relationship with their holy God. Innocent blood had to be sacrificed for the sins of humanity—in this case, the blood of animals. These sacrifices were not a permanent solution to sin, however. They were merely a forerunner of the ultimate sacrifice of Jesus Christ—a sinless Man—for the sins of the world.

THE FIRST TAKING OF HUMAN LIFE

The precious nature of blood continues to unfold to us as we further read the biblical account of the beginning of humanity. Because blood is sacred, it is a cause for judgment if it is spilled wantonly. Tragically, a disregard for human life was manifested shortly after the human race began. Cain was angry when his offering of crops was not accepted. Although God warned Cain that his anger could lead to sin, Cain ignored Him and killed his brother out of jealousy—the first murder committed on earth.

God asked Cain,

What have you done? The voice of your brother's blood cries out to Me from the ground. So now you are cursed from the earth, which has opened its mouth to receive your brother's blood from your hand.
(Genesis 4:10–11)

This incident emphasizes the value of the blood of human beings. The act of murder and the shedding of another person's blood is so terrible an act that when Abel's blood was spilled out on the earth, it "cried out" to God for justice.

The Lord told Moses when He gave him the law,

You shall not pollute the land where you are; for blood defiles the land, and no atonement can be made for the land, for the blood that is shed on it, except by the blood of him who shed it.   (Numbers 35:33)

Since life is in the blood, only blood can make amends for the taking of life. God told the Israelites,

HUMANITY IS IN A FALLEN
STATE. WHILE MOST OF US ARE
NOT MURDERERS, EVERY ONE
OF US DEMONSTRATES OUR
FALLEN NATURE IN THAT WE
HAVE ALL MISSED THE MARK.
WE HAVE ALL SINNED, IN ONE
WAY OR ANOTHER. NONE OF US
HAS LIVED A PERFECT LIFE. NO
MATTER HOW GOOD-NATURED WE
ARE OR HOW LOVING AND GIVING
WE MAY BE, WE STILL HAVE
INSTANCES OF SELFISHNESS,
JEALOUSY, OR OTHER VICES.

*For the life of the flesh is in the blood, and I have given it to you upon the altar to make atonement for your souls; **for it is the blood that makes atonement for the soul**…for it is the life of all flesh. Its blood sustains its life. Therefore I said to the children of Israel, "You shall not eat the blood of any flesh, for the life of all flesh is its blood. Whoever eats it shall be cut off."*
(Leviticus 17:11, 14, emphasis added)

Sadly, from the time of Cain until today, human beings have continued to shed one another's blood, destroying those made in the very image of God and ignoring the pricelessness of life. The Old Testament prophet Micah described the desperate state of mankind in this way:

The faithful man has perished from the earth, and there is no one upright among men. They all lie in wait for blood; every man hunts his brother with a net. That they may successfully do evil with both hands; the prince asks for gifts, the judge seeks a bribe, and the great man utters his evil desire; so they scheme together. The best of them is like a brier; the most upright is sharper than a thorn hedge.
(Micah 7:2–4)

Humanity is in a fallen state. While most of us are not murderers, every one of us demonstrates our fallen nature in that we have all missed the mark. We have all sinned, in one way or another. None of us has lived a perfect life. No matter how good-natured we are or how loving and giving we may be, we still have instances of selfishness, jealousy, or other vices. In addition, the fallen nature of this world is demonstrated by the fact that suffering, in some form, is the common lot of all people. Things are not right for us personally, and they are not right in the world.

Not only has human life become cheap in many people's eyes, but humanity's understanding of and reaction to blood itself has been distorted. Blood seems to have a strong effect on human beings: It either repulses a person or appeals to him. Many are squeamish at the sight of blood. Others are morbidly curious about it, fascinated with blood itself and with its symbols.

Many people have attempted to understand the unusual power of blood to intrigue. Hollywood and the media understand the drawing power of bloodshed and gore. People involved in the occult use blood in various rites and ceremonies as a central part of their false religions. These things appeal to man's base instincts. The fact is that our enemy, Satan, understands the sacredness of blood and causes people to misuse it for his perverse, evil purposes.

After the fall of humanity, the evil and violence on earth became so bad that, by the time of Noah, God destroyed all the people in the world with a flood—except for Noah and his family, who were righteous in God's eyes. The Bible says,

> Then the LORD saw that **the wickedness of man was great** in the earth, and that **every intent of the thoughts of his heart was only evil continually.** And the LORD was sorry that He had made man on the earth, and He was grieved in His heart.
>
> (Genesis 6:5–6, emphasis added)

ATTACKING THE IMAGE OF GOD

Through God's instructions to Noah and his family after the flood, we come to understand even more about the nature of blood and why it is so precious. In Genesis 9:6, God explained to Noah and his family that every person's life and blood are priceless because we are made in His image: *"Whoever sheds man's blood, by man his blood shall be shed; for in the image of God He made man."* Even the lives of fallen human beings are valued in the sight of God because we were created in His image and any violation of our lives must be accounted for.

ATONEMENT NEEDED

Do you think that when Adam and Eve disobeyed God, they knew that they would unleash a bloodbath on the earth?

Undoubtedly not, but that is what happened when they disregarded Him and His ways. We have experienced thousands of years of bloodshed through wars, massacres, genocide, and murder that ultimately resulted from that first disobedience. It is not just physical bloodshed that is the problem; rebellion against God is the overall cause, and it must be atoned for. As Jesus told us,

> *You have heard that it was said to those of old, "You shall not murder, and whoever murders will be in danger of the judgment." But I say to you that whoever is angry with his brother without a cause shall be in danger of the judgment.*   (Matthew 5:21–22)

All sin, including murder, leads to spiritual death and can be atoned for only by blood sacrifice. The price is high, and it must be paid. Sin must be dealt with. Bloodshed must be paid for by blood. Many centuries ago, these truths were evident in the Old Testament prophecies and practices. The sacrificial system was God's way of illustrating for us what the death of Christ—the shedding of His blood—would accomplish for us in restoring us to God and giving us eternal life.

3

THE BLOOD IN OLD TESTAMENT SACRIFICES

*"Without shedding of blood there
is no remission."*
—Hebrews 9:22

The necessity of the shedding of blood for reconciliation with God stands at the very center of the Christian message of redemption. From the first stories of Genesis to the last visions of Revelation, this theme recurs in diverse situations and in a multitude of ways.

Many Bibles have the words of Christ written in red ink. Yet it has been said that the entire Bible was written in red—blood red. This is because there is a "crimson thread" that extends all the way from the skins of the animals God killed to cover the nakedness of Adam and Eve to the Rider of the white horse in the book of Revelation. The Bible calls the name of that Rider *"Faithful and True"* and says that *"He was clothed with a robe dipped in blood, and His name is called The Word of God"* (Revelation 19:11, 13).

Of the several hundred appearances of the word *blood* in the Old Testament, more than one hundred relate to the blood of sacrifices. These sacrifices were a type, or foreshadowing, of the supreme sacrifice of the sinless Christ and of the reconciliation with God provided through His shed blood. While the Old Testament sacrifices needed to be offered daily, yearly, and for specific situations, only His blood was able to atone for the sins of the whole world once and for all.

The sacrificial system practiced by the Jewish people from the time of the Exodus through the rest of the Old Testament is rich in symbolism. The Old Testament sacrifices that Israel offered up to God were defined and explained in exact detail through the commands the Lord gave to Moses on Mt. Sinai. Not only does the sacrificial system convey the strong message that sin must be paid for, but it also expresses the truth that, in the justice of God, only blood can pay the sin price. It prepares the way for us to understand the sacrifice of Christ.

REINFORCING THE PERSONAL COST OF SIN

In the Levitical instructions for carrying out the rituals of sacrifice, blood was prominent. If the people followed God's instructions to the letter, they brought animals for sacrifice from their own flocks and herds rather than buying them from someone else. Only later, when temple worship had become corrupt and its practitioners were merely going through the motions, did the Jews purchase animals for sacrifice within the temple grounds. (See, for example, Mark 11:15.)

In the beginning, however, God's directions were that they were to bring only animals of the highest quality and value that already belonged to them. This requirement reinforced the message of the personal cost of sin.

Many people today, who see dead animals only in supermarkets, neatly packaged, think of the sacrificial act as something abhorrent or despicable. In fact, some have even called the sacrificial system a "slaughterhouse religion." First, we must not forget that the Israelites lived in a culture where people raised their own livestock, and killing animals for food was a routine matter of daily life. Yet a main reason God gave His people this system was so they would understand that sin is costly and must be atoned for. Those who brought offerings to the priests were to grasp the fact that there was a price to pay for having sinned and that one cannot lightly enter into the presence of a holy God.

The sacrifices took place in the tabernacle, and later the temple, following a ritual presentation that was often accompanied by a confession of sin. In this way, the spiritual truth of the significance of sacrifice was meant to hit home to the people. They were to comprehend clearly that blood was necessary for atonement.

THE MEANING OF ATONEMENT

The Hebrew word used most often in the Old Testament for atonement is *kaphar*. The literal meaning of this word is "to cover." The English word *atone* is a construct of "at one," signifying that, as a result of Jesus's actions on our behalf, we are reconciled to, or "at one" with, our heavenly Father. The bloody sacrifice is a covering of sin so that sin no longer stands in the way of our relationship with God.

GOD'S PRESCRIBED SACRIFICES

In the Levitical system, certain offerings were prescribed by God. Among them were animal sacrifices, such as the burnt offering, the sin offering, the guilt (or trespass) offering, and peace offerings, which were always stated in the plural. Peace offerings were further divided into three: the thank (or praise) offering, the votive (or vow) offering, and the freewill offering. There were also vegetable sacrifices, such as the cereal (or "meat") offering.

Let's briefly look at the practices and meanings of these sacrifices, for they reveal much about how God views our relationship with Him and about the atoning sacrifice of the Lamb of God on our behalf.

BURNT OFFERING

The most frequently offered sacrifice was the burnt offering, described in detail in Leviticus 1 and Leviticus 6:8–13. The burnt offering was offered daily in the morning and evening and, on certain days, more frequently. *The Zondervan Pictorial Dictionary* explains, "The purpose of the offering was propitiation, but with this idea was united another, the entire consecration of the worshiper to Jehovah....This was the normal sacrifice of the Israelite in proper covenant relationship with God."[1] Offering a further perspective, *The New Unger's Bible Dictionary* says, "This ritual sets forth Christ offering Himself without spot to God in performing the divine will with joy, even to the point of death."[2]

This sacrifice required a young male animal from the offerer's herd or flock—a bull, ram, lamb, or goat—without any kind of bodily blemish. However, the economic standing of the offerers was taken into consideration, and the very poor could offer birds rather than the more expensive animals.

Unlike the other sacrifices, this one was burned entirely, signifying the person's or congregation's full consecration or surrender to the Lord. That is why it is often called the whole burnt offering. The one bringing the sacrificial animal presented it to the priest at the entrance to the tabernacle (later, the temple). In the process, the offerer would lay his hand on the head of the animal, symbolizing the transmittal of the person's sin to the animal substitute. The offerer himself would take a knife and kill the animal. The attending priest would sprinkle the blood upon the altar. Then the person would cut the sacrifice in pieces and present it to the priest for burning. (See Leviticus 1:3–9.)

SIN OFFERING

The sin offering is described in Leviticus 4:1–35 and Leviticus 6:24–30. Generally, it was made by one who had committed sin without realizing, at the time, that what he had done was sinful. It also applied to sins committed unintentionally rather than actively and deliberately. "It was...the offering among the Hebrews in which the ideas of propitiation and of atonement for sin were most distinctly marked. Its presentation presupposed the consciousness of sin on the part of the person presenting it."[3]

When a sin offering was made for a priest or for the whole congregation of people, the blood of the sacrifice—a young bull—was taken into the Holy Place by the officiating priest and sprinkled seven times in front of the veil of the sanctuary. Some of the blood was placed on the horns of the altar of sweet incense in the tabernacle of meeting. The rest of the blood was poured at the base of the altar of the burnt offering.

If the sin offering was for an individual (other than a priest), the blood of the sacrifice—a female goat—was placed on the horns of the altar of burnt offering, with the remainder poured at the base of the altar.

The fat portions of these sacrifices were burned on the altar. Offerings for priests or the whole congregation were then taken outside the camp and burned. Offerings for individuals were eaten by the priests in the Holy Place. Special instructions applied to the Day of Atonement, which we will review later.

GUILT (TRESPASS) OFFERING

The instructions for the guilt or trespass offering are recorded in Leviticus 5:14–6:7. It differed from the sin offering in that it required not only the usual sacrifice, but also the payment of restitution, either to the offended person or to the priests (if the offense was against God). The offending person had to give back the equivalent of what was taken or lost and add one-fifth of the value to it. "This ritual prefigures Christ's atoning for the damage of sin....It has in view not so much the guilt of sin, which is the aspect of the sin offering, but rather the injury."[4] The sacrifice was offered after the restitution had been made.

PEACE OFFERINGS

As I mentioned earlier, the three peace offerings described in Leviticus 3 are the thank (or praise) offering, the votive (or vow) offering, and the freewill offering. The names indicate the purpose of each: to give thanks for some blessing received, to demonstrate that a vow had been fulfilled, or to express gratitude from a glad heart.

The Zondervan Pictorial Bible Dictionary says, "These were called peace-offerings because they were offered by those who were at peace with God, to express gratitude and obligation to God, and fellowship with Him. They were not commanded to be offered at any set time, except Pentecost (Lev. 23:20), and were presented spontaneously as the feelings of the worshiper prompted (Lev. 19:5)."[5] *Unger's* adds how this offering was a forerunner of Christ: "This ritual portrays Christ as our peace."[6]

Peace offerings were animal sacrifices. The fatty portions were burned on the altar before the Lord and the remaining parts were eaten. The parts of the peace offerings that could be eaten were distributed between the one who brought the offering and the priests who accepted it. Leviticus indicates that the meat from such sacrifices had to be eaten on the same day they were offered in the temple or the next day. (See Leviticus 7:15–17.)

CEREAL ("MEAT") OFFERING

The cereal or "meat" offering was an offering of grain. The King James Version lists this offering as "meat" because, in the days when this version of the Bible was translated, the word *meat* meant what we convey today by the word *meal*. Technically, no flesh was required, although the prescribing verses indicate that the cereal offering often accompanied an animal sacrifice. (See Leviticus 2:1–16 and 6:14–23.) In fact, the cereal offering was made twice daily along with the burnt offerings.

The cereal offering could be brought to the priest in various forms, including cooked cakes or portions of grain. If it were a cooked product, only the finest ingredients could be employed and no leaven or honey was permitted. A token part of it (a handful) was presented to the priest to be burned, and the remainder could be eaten by the priests. The primary purpose of the cereal offering seemed to be to secure or keep the good will of the Lord. Regarding its symbolism in relationship to the Supreme Sacrifice, "this offering exhibits Christ in His human perfections tested by suffering. The fine flour represents the sinless humanity of our Lord. The fire is testing by suffering even unto death."[7]

THE MEANING OF THE SACRIFICE

The significance of the offering of a sacrifice is captured in Leviticus 1:3–4:

He shall offer it of his own free will at the door of the tabernacle of meeting before the LORD. Then he shall put his hand on the head of the burnt offering, and it will be accepted on his behalf to make atonement for him.

A certain painful realization must have stricken the one who brought the sacrifice, for he was bringing an animal of superior value that he had raised from its birth. He knew the reason the animal was dying was that he, the offerer, had sinned. His delivering the animal, laying his hand on its head to confer upon it his own sin, presenting it to the priest—this whole series of acts must have reminded him of the terrible price of sin. The sacrificial victim had to die in order for atonement to be made. This is because the life of the flesh is in the blood, and blood must be shed for the remission of sin.

THE ROLE OF THE PRIEST

An examination of the sacrificial system is not complete without a consideration of the role of the priest. It was the priest's responsibility to make the congregation aware of its sacrificial duties. The ministry of the priest is contrasted with that of the prophet. While the prophet heard from God and announced to the people what God wished them to hear, the priest's main work was to take the sacrifices of the people and present them to God.

We can picture the prophet with his face turned toward God, listening for His revelation, then turning his face toward the people and proclaiming what God has said. In contrast, we can picture the priest with his face turned toward the people, listening for their confession of sin and receiving their offerings, then turning his face toward God and offering their sacrifices to Him.

The job of the priest was to keep the fire burning on the altar and to sprinkle, apply, and/or pour the blood on the altar and other sacred places. It should be pointed out that the priest himself had to make offerings for his own sin, just as the people did, with one exception. While the people could often eat a portion of the sacrifice they brought, the priest could not eat any part of his own sacrifice. Anything that remained after the prescribed parts had been burned on the altar had to be burned by the priest outside the camp. When we look closely at the sacrificial offering of Jesus Himself and the role He fulfilled as the Great High Priest, it will become even more apparent that these Old Testament types are full of meaning for us.

THE TABERNACLE: A PATTERN OF HEAVENLY THINGS

We've talked about the various sacrifices and the role of the priest. Now, let's look at the tabernacle itself (later, the Israelites built the temple for the purpose of worship and sacrifice). The altar of burnt offering was located in the outer court of the tabernacle. Earlier, I mentioned the "horns" of the altar. These were its corners. Inside the tabernacle was the Holy Place, which contained the golden altar of incense.

A veil or curtain separated the Holy Place from the special inner room called the Holy of Holies or Most Holy Place. The most sacred part of the Holy of Holies—to God and to man—was the ark of the covenant, also called the ark of testimony. The ark was a rectangular box about forty-five inches long, twenty-seven inches wide, and twenty-seven inches high. It was made of acacia wood and overlaid with pure gold, inside and outside. The lid to this chest was called the mercy seat or atonement cover.

God instructed Moses to place replicas of two cherubim on each end of the mercy seat, upon which the blood of atonement would be sprinkled. The wings of both were spread forward, and provided a symbolic covering for the atonement. The following are the plans that God gave Moses for the mercy seat.

> *You shall make a mercy seat of pure gold; two and a half cubits shall be its length and a cubit and a half its width. And you shall make two cherubim of gold; of hammered work you shall make them at the two ends of the mercy seat. Make one cherub at one end, and the other cherub at the other end; you shall make the*

cherubim at the two ends of it of one piece with the mercy seat. And the cherubim shall stretch out their wings above, covering the mercy seat with their wings, and they shall face one another; the faces of the cherubim shall be toward the mercy seat. You shall put the mercy seat on top of the ark, and in the ark you shall put the Testimony that I will give you. And there I will meet with you, and I will speak with you from above the mercy seat, from between the two cherubim which are on the ark of the Testimony, about everything which I will give you in commandment to the children of Israel.   (Exodus 25:17–22)

THE DAY OF ATONEMENT

The Day of Atonement has special significance within the sacrificial system. The Hebrew word for atonement in this context is *kippur*. Significantly, the *New American Standard Concordance* says that *kippur* is derived from a Hebrew word meaning "the price of a life."[8]

It should be noted that, although the old Jewish system of animal sacrifices has long been discontinued, the Day of Atonement, called *Yom Kippur* today, is still observed as the most holy day in the Jewish religious year.

The Day of Atonement was anything but a celebration: It was a day of travail and repentance. It was a day when the

Israelites acknowledged their sins before the Lord and their helplessness to put away their sins. In Leviticus 16, it becomes apparent that the day was significant because it presented an opportunity for everyone, from the high priest to the most common citizen, and even the sanctuary itself, to be presented before God for cleansing.

The central aspect of the Day of Atonement was the offering of two male goats. One was presented as a blood sacrifice, and its blood was taken into the Holy of Holies and sprinkled on the mercy seat, where the figures of the winged cherubim represented an approach to the throne of God. It was at the mercy seat that the presence of God was manifested. (See Leviticus 16:2.) Where there is atonement, the presence of God can commune with man.

The high priest placed both of his hands on the head of the other goat, representing the transfer of the sins of the people onto the animal. The goat was then led into the wilderness and turned loose. This goat was called the "scapegoat."

In Hebrew, the word for scapegoat is *azazel*. This word has caused great debate among Bible scholars. Some have believed that Azazel was a demon or representative of Satan. It seems more likely, however, that the word simply reflects another word from which it derives. This Hebrew word, *azal*, means "to remove," denoting that the sin of the people has been removed. In fact, one definition given for *azazel* is "entire removal."[9]

The sacrificed goat, the blood of which was sprinkled on the mercy seat, represents God's covering of sin while the goat that was released into the wilderness represents God's deliverance of His people from sin. Both of them together illustrate the truth that God's atonement is full and complete.

On the Day of Atonement, the high priest first atoned for himself and his household, then for the tabernacle, and then for all of Israel. (See Leviticus 16.) This atonement allowed him to gain standing with God and to present the blood at the mercy seat, which would provide for the sins of the people. When the high priest entered into the Holy of Holies to offer the blood for propitiation, the righteous demands of God upon the sinners were satisfied for a period of one year.

The next year, he had to do it all over again.

IN THE FULLNESS OF TIME

Bible scholars who probe the Old Testament sacrificial system tell us that all the blood shed on Jewish altars through the centuries never took away one sin. Yet God commanded this system in order to provide a "covering" for people's sin until the Supreme Sacrifice would be made, which would forever wash away all sins. "[Jesus] *is the propitiation for our sins: and not for ours only, but also for the sins of the whole world*" (1 John 2:2 KJV).

THE BLOOD OF CHRIST ALONE IS SUFFICIENT TO FULLY ATONE FOR SIN. THE OLD TESTAMENT DAY OF ATONEMENT PREFIGURED THE ONCE-FOR-ALL SACRIFICE THAT JESUS PAID ON THE CROSS. JESUS, OUR GREAT HIGH PRIEST, HAD NO NEED TO OFFER SACRIFICE FOR HIS OWN SINS, BECAUSE HE WAS OUR SINLESS SIN-BEARER.

Even so, every single sacrifice of blood in the Old Testament was a sacred event because of the blood that was shed and poured out on the altar. Each offering was important to God, for each sacrificial animal was an offering, a testimony, and a promise.

- As an offering, each atoning sacrifice covered the sins of the worshiper.

- As a testimony, each sacrifice proclaimed the coming of the true Lamb of God.

- As a promise, each sacrifice pointed to the precious blood of the Lamb of God, which would be sufficient to end all further blood sacrifices.

The blood of Christ alone is sufficient to fully atone for sin. The Old Testament Day of Atonement prefigured the once-for-all sacrifice that Jesus paid on the cross. Jesus, our Great High Priest, had no need to offer sacrifice for His own sins, because He was our sinless Sin-bearer. The sacrifice He made of His own blood was presented by Him in the heavenly Holy of Holies, a sacrifice that never needs to be repeated.

In the heavenly Father's perfect timing, Jesus fulfilled every prophecy and every promise of God when He shed His blood for you and me:

When the fullness of the time had come, God sent forth His Son, born of a woman, born under the law, to redeem those who were under the law, that we might receive the adoption as sons.   (Galatians 4:4–5)

4

THE ONE SACRIFICE

"By one sacrifice he has made perfect forever those
who are being made holy."
—Hebrews 10:14 (NIV)

Everywhere I go today, I meet people who are experiencing a sense of lostness. Not only do they lack meaning in their lives, but they also feel a kind of desolation in their souls. Throughout the centuries, most men and women have felt this same deep sense of being lost and alone. At times, they feel as if they are a million miles away from God.

Regardless of their religions and whether or not they will admit it, many people seek to make peace with God through sacrifice and works. Even pagans in foreign lands instinctively seek reconciliation with deity. Whatever gods people around the world may worship, their worship usually involves some kind of sacrificial ritual to gain the gods' favor. People's consciences seem to cry out for a way to reach their Creator.

This sense of lostness comes from the fact that they are unable to be reconciled to God on their own. They need a Mediator. Let's look more closely at why Jesus's sacrifice is the only way we can be restored to God.

THE INADEQUACY OF THE OLD COVENANT

Although the Mosaic sacrificial system was given to the Israelites, its truths are applicable to all people. The sacrifices, the priests, the mercy seat in the Holy of Holies, and other aspects of the tabernacle were only earthly copies of the heavenly reality that had not yet been manifested. (See Hebrews 8:4–5.)

> *Into the second part* [of the tabernacle] *the high priest went alone once a year, not without blood, which he offered for himself and for the people's sins committed in ignorance; the Holy Spirit indicating this, that the way into the Holiest of All was not yet made manifest*

while the first tabernacle was still standing. It was symbolic for the present time in which both gifts and sacrifices are offered which cannot make him who performed the service perfect in regard to the conscience; concerned only with foods and drinks, various washings, and fleshly ordinances imposed until the time of reformation. (Hebrews 9:7–10)

The first covenant, based on people's obedience to the law and the offering of animal sacrifices, was inferior to the second covenant that came through Jesus Christ and is based on grace and faith. *"For the law was given through Moses, but grace and truth came through Jesus Christ"* (John 1:17).

The old covenant of the law could never do the job of reconciling man to God and cleansing him from the awful stain of sin that has blighted the human race. Its purpose was to remind people of their sin while demonstrating the consequences of sin.

The Lord gave a clear, concise, and strongly worded proclamation about the consequences of sin when He said through the prophet Ezekiel, *"The soul who sins shall die"* (Ezekiel 18:20). God's justice and holiness would not allow Him to forgive sin by simply issuing a divine decree. He does not merely look down and say, "Your intentions were good, so it's all right," or "Because you've done a lot of good things this past week, I'll overlook your sins and let them slide by this time."

Once I had a vision of God in His purity and majesty. The pristine sight was truly awesome. As wave after wave of His glory swept over me, I had a sense of the true holiness of God. I came to realize that God's holiness will not allow Him to overlook sin. The Bible says, *"For the wages of sin is death"* (Romans 6:23). Yet my death or your death will not suffice to pay the debt we owe God or to atone for our sins. Neither the blood of animals nor any human effort at salvation is enough. The only sacrifice qualified to pay for our sins and reconcile us to God is the perfect blood that Jesus shed on the cross.

The sacrificial system is also meant to point people to their need for reconciliation and communion with God. If the sinner himself is not to die for his sins and is not to remain separated from God, then a representative must bear the sinner's death. This is the heart of the message of the sacrificial system.

THE NECESSITY OF THE NEW COVENANT

One of the great deficiencies of the sacrificial system was its temporariness. A sacrifice availed for a sin, but if a sin was repeated, a new sacrifice had to be presented at the altar. Perhaps no fuller explanation of the necessity of the blood sacrifice of Christ is offered than in the following passages:

For if that first covenant had been faultless, then no place would have been sought for a second.

(Hebrews 8:7)

For it is not possible that the blood of bulls and goats could take away sins. Therefore, when He came into the world, He said: "Sacrifice and offering You did not desire, but a body You have prepared for Me."… Previously saying, "Sacrifice and offering, burnt offerings, and offerings for sin You did not desire, nor had pleasure in them" (which are offered according to the law), then He said, "Behold, I have come to do Your will, O God." He takes away the first that He may establish the second. (Hebrews 10:4–5, 8–9)

THE BLOOD OF JESUS PAID THE PRICE

The Old Testament high priest and the tabernacle were cleansed ceremonially with blood. On the Day of Atonement every year, the high priest went into the Holy of Holies with a basin of blood to sprinkle afresh the mercy seat. This was a type or forerunner of what Jesus would do through His death on the cross.

It was necessary that the copies of the things in the heavens should be purified with these, but the heavenly things themselves with better sacrifices than these.

> *For Christ has not entered the holy places made with hands, which are copies of the true, but into heaven itself, now to appear in the presence of God for us.*
>
> (Hebrews 9:23–24)

Jesus's death on the cross was superior to the blood of thousands upon thousands of sacrificial animals. (See Micah 6:7.) His high priestly work in mediating between God and man is superior to all the priests of all the ages combined.

> *But Christ came as High Priest of the good things to come, with the greater and more perfect tabernacle not made with hands, that is, not of this creation. Not with the blood of goats and calves, but with His own blood He entered the Most Holy Place once for all, having obtained eternal redemption. For if the blood of bulls and goats and the ashes of a heifer, sprinkling the unclean, sanctifies for the purifying of the flesh, how much more shall the blood of Christ, who through the eternal Spirit offered Himself without spot to God, cleanse your conscience from dead works to serve the living God? And for this reason He is the Mediator of the new covenant, by means of death, for the redemption of the transgressions under the first covenant, that those who are called may receive the promise of the eternal inheritance.*
>
> (Hebrews 9:11–15)

In the United States, people ratify agreements with their signatures. Then, we have witnesses sign the agreements that we have made. Finally, we often have the documents notarized. In a spiritual sense, God has verified, ratified, and notarized His agreement with us in blood—the blood of His only begotten Son Jesus Christ.

The blood of the sacrifice served as a propitiation for sin. *"He is the propitiation for our sins: and not for ours only, but also for the sins of the whole world"* (1 John 2:2 KJV). "To propitiate" means to conciliate or appease or make favorably inclined. This was the purpose of the sacrifice of the blood, and it satisfied the requirements of a righteous God. Because of God's great love for us, He provided payment for our sin. The blood of Jesus Christ pays our debt *in full!*

For all have sinned and fall short of the glory of God, and are justified freely by his grace through the redemption that came by Christ Jesus. God presented him as a sacrifice of atonement, through faith in his blood. He did this to demonstrate his justice, because in his forbearance he had left the sins committed beforehand unpunished—he did it to demonstrate his justice at the present time, so as to be just and the one who justifies those who have faith in Jesus.

(Romans 3:24–26 NIV)

Let's take a closer look at how Jesus paid the debt that no one else could pay and made atonement for our sins, enabling us to have eternal life.

HISTORICAL CALVARY

Each year, thousands of tourists visit Jerusalem and walk the streets where Jesus once walked. Tour guides usually lead visitors to the Garden Tomb, which many believe is the place where Jesus arose from the dead. After touring a garden of olive trees, you are led along a path to an observation platform that overlooks the streets of the ancient city of Jerusalem.

Your attention is then immediately drawn to a hill and a cliff to the left of the platform. The cliff has several physical indentations, and its dark shadows give it the unmistakable appearance of a skull. There, the guide tells you, is what is known as Calvary or, in the Hebrew, *Golgotha*.

In Jesus's day, just the mention of Calvary likely struck fear in the hearts of people, especially lawbreakers, for Calvary was a place of execution (in the same way that the electric chair, the gas chamber, or lethal injection causes fear in lawbreakers today). Two thousand years ago, that small hill apparently held an important place in the Roman punitive system. It was one of many sites where the Romans used to carry out capital punishment in the form of crucifixion, one of the most excruciating ways a person can die. Through many torturous hours—even days—of suffering, the condemned person hung between heaven and earth, suspended by nails driven through his flesh.

Atop that relatively small hill, there is a cemetery with various monuments erected in memory of the people buried there. To modern-day Hebrews, Calvary is simply a place to bury the dead. Muslims, the followers of Islam, call it the place where the lesser prophet, Jesus, suffered at the hands of infidels.

To some atheists and secularists, Calvary is the object of jokes, a place of ridicule. To rationalists, Calvary is merely the place where a historical figure named Jesus died. While they may admit that His death was perhaps tragic, they assign no spiritual significance to it. They reason, "He must not have been the Son of God, since God cannot die. If Jesus's body could not be found, then either Jesus did not die but was only badly injured and later regained consciousness, or His disciples stole His body and hid it, afterward claiming that Jesus was resurrected."

Yet, in our heavenly Father's grand design, Calvary was the setting for a world-changing reconciliation between God and humanity. He chose to make that small hill an altar on which the supreme sacrifice would be made. In His divine and mysterious wisdom, He made it the place at which the Son of God shed His blood for the total remission of our sins.

CALVARY WAS THE SETTING
FOR A WORLD-CHANGING
RECONCILIATION BETWEEN
GOD AND HUMANITY. HE CHOSE
TO MAKE THAT SMALL HILL AN
ALTAR ON WHICH THE SUPREME
SACRIFICE WOULD BE MADE. IN
HIS DIVINE AND MYSTERIOUS
WISDOM, HE MADE IT THE PLACE
AT WHICH THE SON OF GOD
SHED HIS BLOOD FOR THE TOTAL
REMISSION OF OUR SINS.

To those who have been forgiven and adopted as children of God, Calvary is hallowed ground. It was there that the Son of God purchased their redemption for all of eternity. It stands forever as a reminder of His sufferings and complete sacrifice on their behalf.

THE SUFFERINGS OF JESUS

AGONY OF SOUL

In chapter one, I mentioned part of the vision of the crucifixion that was revealed to me. God also allowed me to see Jesus in the garden of Gethsemane where He prayed the evening before His death. The Scripture says, *"And being in agony, He prayed more earnestly. Then His sweat became like great drops of blood falling down to the ground"* (Luke 22:44). I heard Jesus tell His disciples, *"My soul is exceedingly sorrowful, even to death"* (Matthew 26:38).

I could see and sense the extreme heaviness of His mission; the weight of it rested upon His shoulders. I believe He was able to endure such a heavy load only because He was the Son of God. He bore the load well! But as the Son of Man, His body was weak, and the stress had begun to take its toll on Him. This was only the beginning, however, for not only would He be put to death, but He would also suffer in many other ways before His crucifixion.

BETRAYAL

In the vision, I encountered many of the central figures involved in the crucifixion. Judas was the worst of all those I saw in the vision because he had been a disciple of Jesus for three-and-a-half years, only to become a traitor because of greed. For only thirty silver coins, Judas betrayed the Lord to those who were trying to kill Him. According to the Bible, Satan had entered into Judas Iscariot's heart. (See Luke 22:3.)

Judas' method of betrayal was horrible and repugnant. He led the chief priests, captains of the temple, and the elders, along with a large crowd of people, to the place where Jesus was praying. As he drew close to Jesus, he kissed Him. Jesus asked, *"Judas, are you betraying the Son of Man with a kiss?"* (Luke 22:48). God's Son suffered the betrayal of one who had been in His closest inner circle.

I also encountered the chief priests and scribes. The Bible says that, just before Jesus was crucified, they *"sought how they might kill [Jesus]"* (Luke 22:2). These religious leaders, who were revered and respected by the Israelite people, became the first voices to call for Jesus's execution. They were the first of the hundreds of people who would eventually make up a bloodthirsty throng clamoring for His crucifixion.

BEATEN AND MOCKED

I also witnessed another part of Jesus's suffering: He was brutally beaten by His captors. I saw this group of religious leaders take Christ to the home of the high priest. They began to interrogate Him. They placed a blindfold on Him and hit Him with their fists. As they did this, they would demand of Him, *"Prophesy! Who is the one who struck You?"* (Luke 22:64). This beating continued through the night.

When dawn came, the religious leaders held a council. They falsely accused Jesus and finally made the pronouncement that He was guilty of blasphemy. Then they took Him to Pilate, the Roman procurator.

When Pilate learned that Jesus was a Galilean, he sent Him to Herod, another Roman official in Jerusalem, because Galilee was under Herod's jurisdiction. After mocking Jesus, Herod put a regal-looking robe on Him and returned Him to Pilate. The Scriptures tell us that on that day, Pilate and Herod, who had been mutual enemies, became friends. (See Luke 23:12.) They were diabolically united in friendship, through the agony they imposed on Jesus.

FALSELY CONDEMNED TO DEATH

Pilate eventually took Jesus before the religious leaders and the people. He was convinced that Jesus was innocent and wanted to free Him. However, he was obviously torn between a desire to do the right thing and a desire to please the people.

I saw Pilate lift his hand before the multitude, and there was silence. Pilate asked the crowd in clear tones what he should do with Jesus. The chief priests stirred up the multitude. Whipped into a frenzied mob, the people began crying aloud, *"Crucify Him!"* (See, for example, Mark 15:13.)

In a futile attempt to rid himself of the responsibility for Jesus's death, Pilate washed his hands in a basin and said, *"You take Him and crucify Him, for I find no fault in Him"* (John 19:6).

Pilate then sentenced Jesus to death and had Him whipped before handing Him over to be crucified. I saw the Roman soldier raise the atrocious whip and strike it fiercely and forcefully across Jesus's back.

CRUELLY SCOURGED

Roman scourging was an extreme form of punishment. The prisoner was bound to a post with his arms tied above his head. The Roman soldiers who did the whipping were typically well practiced in their craft. They were adept at inflicting the maximum pain.

The whip they used was similar to a cat-o'-nine-tails, although, instead of knots, the bands of leather had pieces of jagged metal or shards of bone tied to them. Each blow would bring angry red welts to the surface of the skin immediately. The pieces of metal or shards of bone would lacerate the swollen skin, digging ever deeper into the flesh. When the scourging finally stopped, strips of torn flesh would hang from the person's back, and he would have lost a great amount of blood.

RIDICULED AND ABUSED

Pilate finally turned Jesus over to be executed. The entire garrison of Roman soldiers gathered around Jesus and ridiculed Him because of His claim to be the King of the Jews. They stripped Him, put a scarlet robe around His shoulders, and placed a reed in His hand. Then I saw His tormentors take a long strand of prickly, thorny vines and twist it into a gruesome crown of thorns. Kneeling before Him in irreverence, they gave Him mock homage. The spitting soldiers screamed in His face.

I watched in horror as they placed that sharp crown of thorns on Jesus's head and pushed it down hard. When they tired of this, one of the soldiers grabbed the reed and began beating the thorns deeper into Jesus's scalp! Here is how the Bible describes the gruesome scene:

> When they had twisted a crown of thorns, they put it on His head, and a reed in His right hand. And they

> *bowed the knee before Him and mocked Him, saying,*
> *"Hail, King of the Jews!" Then they spat on Him, and*
> *took the reed and struck Him on the head. And when*
> *they had mocked Him, they took the robe off Him,*
> *put His own clothes on Him, and led Him away to be*
> *crucified.* (Matthew 27:29–31)

Both Pilate and Herod had opportunities to release Jesus when they saw that He had done nothing deserving of death. However, they were swayed by popular opinion, and they would not free Him. Roman soldiers scourged Jesus while the Jewish religious leaders cried, "Crucify Him!" A Roman leader condemned Him to death while the mob cried, "Crucify Him!" (See verses 20, 22–23 NIV.)

All this is what Jesus suffered even before He went to the cross. It grieves my heart to think of the motley crew involved in the events that led to the death of Jesus. The chief priests, the scribes, the Pharisees, and the Sanhedrin Court were all a party to getting the Roman rulers to sentence Jesus to death and to carry out the execution. Together, they incited the mobs of common people in the streets of Jerusalem to cry out for His death.

Jew and Gentile, lord and servant, ruler and peasant—they were all united in calling for the blood of Jesus to be shed. People sometimes debate who was really responsible for the crucifixion of Christ. Yet, if you were to try to establish a culprit, you would be hard-pressed to find a single person or group with more culpability than any other. You could blame Judas, Pilate, the members of the Sanhedrin Court, the Romans, or the mob of people, but it was a joint effort between all of them—and us.

The Scriptures confirm this truth, for it was to pay for our sins that Jesus went to that cross:

> *It is written: "There is none righteous, no, not one; there is none who understands; there is none who seeks after God. They have all turned aside; they have together become unprofitable; there is none who does good, no, not one."*　　(Romans 3:10–12)

No one person or group was more responsible than the others for the death of Christ. Just as all are guilty of sin, so all are responsible for the shedding of Christ's blood on Calvary.

The visions that God gave to me of the crucifixion are just as real in my mind and heart as ever. The finger of God has etched the scenes of His death there. Two thousand years have passed since that terrible day. We are two millennia separated from its horrors. Still, in my heart, I know that you and I are as responsible for Jesus's death as those who actually carried it out.

CRUCIFIED

The concept of the crucifixion that many people have is of Jesus hanging on the cross. They know that is how He died, but they are not familiar with the true agony of such a death.

In the vision, I saw four men holding Jesus's limbs while a fifth soldier drove the spikes through His flesh and into the cross. Jesus's limbs were not stretched out completely, but He was allowed a little room for movement. I learned later that this was not out of pity, but to make His sufferings more extreme.

When a person was suspended on a cross, his weight would come to rest on the nails in his hands and feet. The weight pulling on the nails in his hands would soon become unbearable, so he would have to push himself upward to relieve the pain in his hands. Yet this would push upon the painful nails in his feet. When this became too painful, He would again have to let his weight hang on his hands. Hours and days of this merciless cycle produced excruciating agony.

Every movement Jesus made would also have scraped the torn and tattered flesh of His back across the rough, splintered texture of the cross. There was no comfort, only deepening levels of pain.

His chest and abdominal muscles—the parts of the body that control breathing—would essentially become paralyzed while he hung in that position. So the condemned man had no choice but to once again push on the nails in his feet to relieve the strain and catch his breath.

Ultimately, death usually came to a crucifixion victim through suffocation. The person would grow weaker as time passed, and a final horror would overtake him. Exhausted, the crucified man would become too weak to push himself up to relieve the pain in his hands, and he would find himself unable to breathe.

Added to all the above was the additional mocking that Jesus underwent even while He was in such physical agony:

[The soldiers] *divided His garments and cast lots. And the people stood looking on. But even the rulers with them sneered, saying, "He saved others; let Him save Himself if He is the Christ, the chosen of God." The soldiers also mocked Him, coming and offering Him sour wine, and saying, "If You are the King of the Jews, save Yourself." And an inscription also was written over Him in letters of Greek, Latin, and Hebrew: This Is The King of the Jews. Then one of the criminals who were hanged blasphemed Him, saying, "If You are the Christ, save Yourself and us."*

(Luke 23:34–39)

AS HE HUNG ON THE CROSS,
JESUS FELT THE EXCRUCIATING
WEIGHT OF THE SINS OF EVERY
PERSON WHO HAS EVER LIVED.
WE NEED TO REMEMBER
THAT JESUS CHRIST NEVER
COMMITTED A SIN AND THAT ALL
OUR SIN AND EVIL CAME TO REST
ON HIM AT ONE TIME.

Again, the crucifixion process could last for days. If the officials wanted to hasten the death of a crucified person, however, his legs were broken so that he could no longer push on the nails in his feet and thus catch his breath. Jesus was crucified alongside the two criminals, and the religious leaders did not want their bodies to stay on the crosses during the special Sabbath that was to be observed the next day. Therefore, they asked Pilate to grant permission for their legs to be broken. He agreed, but when the soldiers came to Jesus, they saw that He was already dead, so they did not break His legs. (See John 19:31–33.)

To ensure that Jesus was dead, however, a Roman soldier thrust a spear into His side, and out of the wound came both blood and water, a sign of death.[1] The Bible tells us,

> *These things were done that the Scripture should be fulfilled, "Not one of His bones shall be broken." And again another Scripture says, "They shall look on Him whom they pierced."*　　　(John 19:36–37)

The horrors of the crucifixion must have been even worse than the terrible suffering I witnessed in my visions. We must always keep in mind that Jesus endured these sufferings for us so that we can be forgiven, restored to a relationship with God, and enjoy abundant and eternal life.

BURDENED WITH THE WEIGHT OF SIN

Jesus volunteered His body, mind, and spirit to the suffering of the cross. Some people consider only the physical suffering He went through. Jesus endured terrible physical pain, but it was probably less painful than the other agony He experienced.

As He hung on the cross, Jesus felt the excruciating weight of the sins of every person who has ever lived. We need to remember that Jesus Christ never committed a sin and that all our sin and evil came to rest on Him at one time. This would be more than any normal person could endure. Also, because God is holy, and sin is abhorrent to Him, the Father withdrew from His Son for the first time ever when Jesus was on the cross. He experienced the desolation of separation from God, just as the rest of mankind has. Jesus was completely alone!

JESUS FULFILLED THE REQUIREMENTS OF AN ATONING SACRIFICE

A SACRIFICE OF PRICELESS VALUE

In the last chapter, we saw that someone who offered a sacrifice under the old covenant had to present an animal or vegetable product of value that personally belonged to him. In making the supreme sacrifice on our behalf, Jesus offered the most precious thing that belonged to Him—His very life.

My Father loves Me, because I lay down My life that I may take it again. No one takes it from Me, but I lay it down of Myself. I have power to lay it down, and I have power to take it again. This command I have received from My Father.   (John 10:17–18)

Christ was not merely a victim of hateful and jealous men, as some believe. Rather, He consciously and willingly *gave up* His life for us. The cross is the centerpiece of God's eternal plan of redemption. Our heavenly Father not only foresaw Calvary, but He also arranged it. Wicked men, no matter how many in number or strength, could never have nailed the Son of God to the cross without the heavenly Father's express permission and the Son's willingness.

A PURE SACRIFICE

Recall also that the sacrifices of the Mosaic system had to be without blemish. Jesus, as our ultimate Sacrifice and Substitute, also had to be totally pure, and He was sinless before God when He offered Himself as our substitute. Many Scriptures testify to His purity and holiness before God and the world, such as the following:

[Jesus said,] *"Can any of you prove me guilty of sin? If I am telling the truth, why don't you believe me?"*

(John 8:46 NIV)

> [Jesus] *committed no sin, nor was deceit found in His mouth.* (1 Peter 2:22)

> *He was manifested to take away our sins, and in Him there is no sin.* (1 John 3:5)

The blood of Jesus is perfect. It is the blood of God's only begotten Son, the God-man, Christ Jesus.

> *Christ Jesus…, being in the form of God, did not consider it robbery to be equal with God, but made Himself of no reputation, taking the form of a bond-servant, and coming in the likeness of men. And being found in appearance as a man, He humbled Himself and became obedient to the point of death, even the death of the cross.* (Philippians 2:5–8)

Christ's blood represents the perfect and completed sacrifice of Himself, which was offered for the sins of the world. Everything about Christ's life was pure—it did not have a single spot or stain of sin. His obedience to God was perfect. He was the only acceptable Sacrifice that could atone for the sins of the people.

> *You were not redeemed with corruptible things, like silver or gold…but with the precious blood of Christ, as of a lamb without blemish and without spot. He*

indeed was foreordained before the foundation of the world.   (1 Peter 1:18–20)

A SACRIFICE BROUGHT OUTSIDE THE CITY

In addition, Jesus satisfied the requirements of an atoning sacrifice in that He was crucified outside the city of Jerusalem. As the Scripture says,

For the bodies of those animals, whose blood is brought into the sanctuary by the high priest for sin, are burned outside the camp. Therefore Jesus also, that He might sanctify the people with His own blood, suffered outside the gate.   (Hebrews 13:11–12)

The greatest donation of blood in history took place on the cross of Calvary two thousand years ago. Only the blood of Jesus can give a transfusion of eternal life! The blood that was shed on that day has been sufficient for the salvation of every sinner ever born and will continue to be effective until the end of time.

A SUBSTITUTIONARY SACRIFICE

Another major way that Jesus fulfilled the requirements of an atoning sacrifice is that His death was completely substitutionary. It was effected to satisfy God's demand for

WHEN WE TALK ABOUT THE
DEATH OF JESUS CHRIST AS
SUBSTITUTIONARY, THIS MEANS
THAT JESUS CHRIST DIED *IN THE
PLACE OF* SINNERS. THE WORD
SUBSTITUTIONARY IS NOT FOUND
IN THE BIBLE, JUST AS THE
WORD *EVANGELISM* IS NOT FOUND
THERE. BUT THE CONCEPT
IS ONE THAT IS REPEATED
THROUGHOUT THE SCRIPTURES.

———————————

righteousness and justice. His blood completely satisfied that demand and effectively put away sin.

When we talk about the death of Jesus Christ as substitutionary, this means that Jesus Christ died *in the place of* sinners. The word *substitutionary* is not found in the Bible, just as the word *evangelism* is not found there. But the concept is one that is repeated throughout the Scriptures.

When Jesus atoned for sin, He stood in the place of guilty men and women. Thus, God the Father planned for Jesus *"who knew no sin to be sin for us, that we might become the righteousness of God in Him"* (2 Corinthians 5:21).

Again, the death of the Lord Jesus Christ was not the punishment of a criminal or the death of a martyr. It was substitutionary. *"For Christ also suffered once for sins, the just for the unjust, that He might bring us to God, being put to death in the flesh but made alive by the Spirit"* (1 Peter 3:18).

Jesus had no sins of His own. He died for us, in place of us, on behalf of us. He died for us all, taking the punishment that we deserved.

In Hebrews 9:5, the Greek word translated *"mercy seat,"* referring to the place of God's presence in the tabernacle, is the same word that is used for *propitiation*. It is altogether proper to render it in this way because the law required death for sin, and when the blood was placed on the mercy seat, it was a demonstration that death had taken place and the satisfactory price had been paid.

The sacrifice of Jesus's blood is entirely sufficient to purge our sins and give us new life. Hebrews tells us,

> *We have been sanctified through the offering of the body of Jesus Christ once for all....For by one offering He has perfected forever those who are being sanctified.* (Hebrews 10:10, 14)

One of the great object lessons of Scripture that reveals the efficacy of the substitutionary blood of Jesus is the story of the Passover. Egypt's refusal to obey God resulted in His decision to require the life of every firstborn Egyptian. God's plan to keep death from affecting the firstborn children of the Israelites was called the Passover.

Each Hebrew family was to kill a lamb and apply its blood above the entrance and on either side of the doors to their homes. Even those many centuries before the New Testament era, the sign of the cross would be efficacious in keeping the curse of death at bay.

For hundreds of years, Jewish families repeated the Passover observance yearly as a constant reminder of the power of God's plan for deliverance. Whether they realized it or not, every time they celebrated the Passover, they were, in effect, prophesying of the day when the Lamb of God would shed His blood for all people.

Spiritually speaking, Jesus's blood can be applied to our hearts to save us from spiritual death and God's wrath. It is no coincidence that the final meal Jesus ate with His disciples, when He taught them the significance of the broken bread and the cup, was in connection with the annual observance of Passover. When Jesus was introduced by John the Baptist at the Jordan River, John called Him *"the Lamb of God who takes away the sin of the world"* (John 1:29). The apostle Paul wrote in 1 Corinthians 5:7, *"Christ, our Passover, was sacrificed for us."*

The cross still destroys the power of death. Just as the first Passover was a celebration of deliverance, the blood today is a sign of God's love and forgiveness and His power to deliver us from both the penalty and power of sin. Praise God that Jesus is our Passover!

JESUS'S DEATH WAS THE ULTIMATE AND FINAL SACRIFICE

The Scriptures say that Jesus Christ offered Himself as a sacrifice *"once for all"* (Hebrews 10:10). This means that, unlike the sacrifices under the law, Jesus's death requires no repetition. It was a sacrifice for the sins of the world for all time. Salvation is complete. It requires nothing else but faith in the atoning merit of the sacrifice and the yielding of one's life to Jesus Christ.

> *For Christ has not entered the holy places made with hands, which are copies of the true, but into heaven itself, now to appear in the presence of God for us; not that He should offer Himself often, as the high priest enters the Most Holy Place every year with blood of another; He then would have had to suffer often since the foundation of the world; but now, once at the end of the ages, He has appeared to put away sin by the sacrifice of Himself. And as it is appointed for men to die once, but after this the judgment, so Christ was offered once to bear the sins of many.*
>
> (Hebrews 9:24–28)

Again, the new covenant through Jesus is not temporal but eternal:

> *Every priest stands ministering daily and offering repeatedly the same sacrifices, which can never take away sins. But this Man, after He had offered one sacrifice for sins forever, sat down at the right hand of God, from that time waiting till His enemies are made His footstool. For by one offering He has per-fected forever those who are being sanctified....[The Lord said,] "Their sins and their lawless deeds I will*

remember no more." Now where there is remission of
these, there is no longer an offering for sin.

(Hebrews 10:11–14, 17–18)

SEVEN BLOOD OFFERINGS

In my vision of the death of Christ, I saw the different ways in which Jesus shed His blood as the ultimate Sacrifice. While reading the book of Leviticus, I came across this intriguing Scripture:

[The high priest] *shall take some of the blood of the*
bull and sprinkle it with his finger on the mercy seat on
the east side; and before the mercy seat he shall sprin-
kle some of the blood with his finger seven times.

(Leviticus 16:14)

Since the Old Testament sacrificial system prefigured New Testament reality, I believe that this rite was an allegory of the seven times Jesus would shed His blood on our behalf during His sufferings.

SWEAT LIKE DROPS OF BLOOD

First, Jesus sweat blood when He prayed to the Father in the garden of Gethsemane about His coming death. He prayed to God the Father, "*If it is Your will, take this cup away from Me; nevertheless not My will, but Yours, be done*" (Luke 22:42).

Perhaps when it came time for Jesus's pure, sinless body to become sin for us, He recoiled at the idea in horror. *"And being in agony, He prayed more earnestly. Then His sweat became like great drops of blood falling down to the ground"* (Luke 23:44).

STRUCK IN THE FACE

Second, Jesus shed blood when He was struck in the face. *"Then they spat in His face and beat Him; and others struck Him with the palms of their hands"* (Matthew 26:67). The prophet Micah had predicted, *"They will strike the judge of Israel with a rod on the cheek"* (Micah 5:1). Because of the abuse He received, the prophet Isaiah said, *"His visage was marred more than any man, and His form more than the sons of men"* (Isaiah 52:14). In the visions God allowed me to see, there was not an inch of His face that was not covered with blood.

SCOURGING

Third, Jesus shed His precious blood when they lashed His back with an angry whip. *"When [Pilate] had scourged Jesus, he delivered Him to be crucified"* (Matthew 27:26). The prophet Isaiah had predicted concerning the Messiah, *"I gave My back to those who struck Me"* (Isaiah 50:6).

PIERCING THORNS

Fourth, Jesus shed blood when the soldiers put the crown of thorns on His head and beat it into His scalp with a club.

The large thorns pierced his flesh, and his head wounds must have bled profusely. *"When they had twisted a crown of thorns, they put it on His head....Then they spat on Him, and took the reed and struck Him on the head"* (Matthew 27:29–30).

BEARD PLUCKED OUT

Fifth, adding insult and increasing injury, Jesus's captors plucked out His beard. Isaiah prophesied, *"I gave...My cheeks to those who plucked out the beard; I did not hide My face from shame and spitting"* (Isaiah 50:6).

CRUCIFIXION

Sixth, Jesus shed His blood when He was crucified. His cry of anguish from the Word of God is, *"They pierced My hands and My feet"* (Psalm 22:16). Precious, sinless blood ran down from His hands and feet as He hung on the cross and gave His all for us.

PIERCED WITH A SPEAR

Finally, Jesus shed His precious blood when the soldier rammed a spear into His side to see if He was dead. *"One of the soldiers pierced His side with a spear, and immediately blood and water came out"* (John 19:34). This act may have been the fulfillment of the prophecy, *"They will look on Me whom they pierced"* (Zechariah 12:10).

THE REST OF THE STORY

For all other men who have been crucified, the story ended when their hearts stopped beating. There was nothing left to do but retrieve and bury the bodies. But Jesus Christ was not any other man. He was the Son of God. There had never been another man like this Man nor would there ever be another like Him.

Jesus was God Himself in human flesh. As God, He was present at the creation of the world, and He was a participant in that event.

In the beginning was the Word, and the Word was with God, and the Word was God. He was in the beginning with God. All things were made through Him, and without Him nothing was made that was made. (John 1:1–3)

Through Jesus, all the stars were put in their ordered places, and the planets were set in their orbit around the sun. He spoke, and the firmament was created, and the waters were parted from the land. Through Him, the grass of the field flourished. He caused the trees to bear fruit. He made the seas teem with life, and He gave the birds their ability to fly.

Jesus was there when the heavenly Father formed Adam from the dust of the ground. He was there when the Father breathed life into Adam, making humanity greater than the beasts of the fields or the birds of the air. He saw the Father cause a great sleep to fall on Adam, then take a single rib from his side and fashion it into a woman.

Jesus also witnessed the tragic entrance of sin into the world, and He willingly came to earth to offer Himself as an atonement for humanity's sins. For this reason He came into the world. For this reason He lived His life. For this reason He offered up His life for us and then was resurrected in glory.

JESUS'S BLOOD "SPEAKS"

The Bible says that *"the blood of sprinkling...speaks better things than that of Abel"* (Hebrews 12:24). Remember that, when Cain killed Abel, God told him, *"The voice of your brother's blood cries out to Me from the ground"* (Genesis 4:10)? Abel's blood rightfully cried out for retribution. Yet Jesus's blood speaks of *"better things"* than retribution.

What are those things? His blood speaks of mercy, forgiveness, and reconciliation. James, the brother of Christ, who was a witness to the events surrounding Jesus's death on the cross, wrote, *"Mercy triumphs over judgment"* (James 2:13).

When Jesus's blood "speaks"—

+ the troubled conscience is at rest

+ the broken heart is healed

+ the tormenting doubt is silenced

+ the trembling fear is quelled

The blood of Christ also speaks for us *"behind the veil"* (Hebrews 6:19) where it has been placed on the heavenly mercy seat. The voice of Jesus's blood of mercy is heard in glory more sweetly and loudly than the voices of all the angels around the throne of God.

His blood pleads louder for you in heaven than all your sins can plead against you on earth.

> *He, because He continues forever, has an unchange-able priesthood. Therefore He is also able to save to the uttermost those who come to God through Him, since He always lives to make intercession for them.*
>
> (Hebrews 7:24–25)

JESUS'S BLOOD MUST BE APPLIED

The blood of Jesus is also the *"blood of sprinkling"* (Hebrews 12:24). David Wilkerson explains,

> This isn't a physical sprinkling; rather, it is a legal, spiritual transaction. He sprinkles the blood on our hearts in response to our faith. And until we truly believe in the power of His sacrifice at

Calvary, the blood of Jesus cannot produce any effect upon our souls![2]

This means that Jesus's blood is applied blood—applied to our hearts and lives, bringing forgiveness, peace, and deliverance. The blood has no practical benefit to us unless it is applied to our consciences, just as the blood of the Passover lamb could not have benefited the Israelite in Egypt if it had not been sprinkled upon the doorposts and lintel of his house. God told His people, *"And when I **see the blood**, I will pass over you"* (Exodus 12:13, emphasis added).

I hope we have the eyes to see and the wisdom to accept God's great act of redeeming love in the sacrifice of the Lord Jesus Christ! Today, not only do many people look with revulsion on the shedding of blood that formed such an essential part of the Old Testament sacrificial system, but they also consider with equal distaste the New Testament teaching concerning Christ's blood. They abhor many of the gospel songs and hymns that emphasize the necessity and power of the blood of Christ. They don't like preachers who preach on the effectiveness of the blood.

Those who scorn the shed blood of Christ have their eyes blinded to the Word of God, to the holiness of God, and to the dreadful and radical nature of sin. Sin is a terrible reality, and it calls for a radical cure. Substitutionary death is the only means to life.

THIS MEANS THAT JESUS'S BLOOD
IS APPLIED BLOOD—APPLIED
TO OUR HEARTS AND LIVES,
BRINGING FORGIVENESS, PEACE,
AND DELIVERANCE. THE BLOOD
HAS NO PRACTICAL BENEFIT
TO US UNLESS IT IS APPLIED TO
OUR CONSCIENCES, JUST AS THE
BLOOD OF THE PASSOVER LAMB
COULD NOT HAVE BENEFITED
THE ISRAELITE IN EGYPT IF IT
HAD NOT BEEN SPRINKLED
UPON THE DOORPOSTS AND
LINTEL OF HIS HOUSE.

The founder of a religious cult that denies the deity of Jesus Christ said that the blood of Christ was no more effective when it was poured out on Calvary than it was in the veins of the living Jesus. But we know that *"without shedding of blood there is no remission"* (Hebrews 9:22). The blood of Jesus Christ was poured out because only through it could we receive life.

WORTHY IS THE LAMB

In one of my visions of heaven, I heard the angels in heaven shouting about Him, *"Worthy is the Lamb who was slain to receive power and riches and wisdom, and strength and honor and glory and blessing!"* (Revelation 5:12). Heaven was shouting and rejoicing because of the momentous significance of Christ's sacrifice.

Amid these shouts and praises, I heard the singing of the people of God. It was the grandest, most eloquent, most melodious singing I have ever heard. Like the sound *"of many waters"* (Revelation 19:6), it seemed to soar and surge and reverberate across the universe. There was no corner where the beautiful song was not heard. What song did they sing?

You are worthy to take the scroll, and to open its seals; for You were slain, and have redeemed us to God by Your blood out of every tribe and tongue and people and nation, and have made us kings and priests to our God; and we shall reign on the earth.

(Revelation 5:9–10)

Likewise, believers through the ages echo, with great joy, the sentiments expressed in the words of this old hymn:

I hear the Savior say,
"Thy strength indeed is small,
Child of weakness, watch and pray,
Find in Me thine all in all."

For nothing good have I
Whereby Thy grace to claim—
I'll wash my garments white
In the blood of Calv'ry's Lamb.

Jesus paid it all,
All to Him I owe;
Sin had left a crimson stain,
He washed it white as snow.[3]

Praise God for the eternal power of the blood of the lamb!

5

THE BLOOD OF THE NEW COVENANT

"He is the Mediator of the new covenant, by means of death, for the redemption of the transgressions under the first covenant, that those who are called may receive the promise of the eternal inheritance."
—Hebrews 9:15

With Christ's ultimate sacrifice, a new covenant was established between God and His people. This new covenant, which replaced the old one that had been entered into long ago when Moses sprinkled blood on the Israelites at the foot of Mount Sinai, was inaugurated by the blood of Jesus Christ at the base of Calvary.

The writer of Hebrews repeated what the Lord had foretold through the prophet Jeremiah about this new covenant:

> *Behold, the days are coming, says the* Lord, *when I will make a **new covenant** with the house of Israel and with the house of Judah; not according to the covenant that I made with their fathers in the day when I took them by the hand to lead them out of the land of Egypt; because they did not continue in My covenant, and I disregarded them, says the* Lord. *For this is the covenant that I will make with the house of Israel after those days, says the* Lord: **I will put My laws in their mind and write them on their hearts; and I will be their God, and they shall be My people.***
>
> (Hebrews 8:8–10, emphasis added)

The new covenant gives us an internal love for God and His ways rather than only an external compliance with His Word. In addition, when we accept Jesus Christ as Lord and Savior and commit ourselves to Him, we can be assured that our covenant-keeping God will always keep His Word. He will be our God, and we will be His people.

Jesus said, *"This is My blood of the new covenant, which is shed for many for the remission of sins"* (Matthew 26:28). The covenant that God has with us is sealed by the blood of Jesus. Without the shedding of His blood, there could be no ratification of the covenant. It would not be valid. Because of His blood, however, we can receive all the promises of this new covenant. The Bible is the testament that reveals to us what God has given to us in Christ. In coming chapters, we will look at the many blessings that have been granted us through the blood of Jesus.

JESUS OUR GREAT HIGH PRIEST

Jesus was not only the Sacrifice for our sins, but He was also the Great High Priest who took the offering of His precious blood to the mercy seat of God. *"Now [Jesus] has obtained a more excellent ministry, inasmuch as He is also Mediator of a better covenant, which was established on better promises"* (Hebrews 8:6).

The writer of Hebrews understood clearly the role of Christ as Mediator. He explained the superiority of the new covenant of blood and of the new Deliverer:

Not with the blood of goats and calves, but with His own blood He entered the Most Holy Place once for all, having obtained eternal redemption. For if the blood of bulls and goats and the ashes of a heifer,

THE COVENANT THAT GOD HAS
WITH US IS SEALED BY THE
BLOOD OF JESUS. WITHOUT THE
SHEDDING OF HIS BLOOD,
THERE COULD BE NO
RATIFICATION OF THE COVENANT.
IT WOULD NOT BE VALID. BECAUSE
OF HIS BLOOD, HOWEVER, WE
CAN RECEIVE ALL THE PROMISES
OF THIS NEW COVENANT.

*sprinkling the unclean, sanctifies for the purifying of
the flesh, how much more shall the blood of Christ,
who through the eternal Spirit offered Himself without spot to God, cleanse your conscience from dead
works to serve the living God?* (Hebrews 9:12–14)

The new covenant does not just cover sin. It actually
cleanses our consciences and frees us to live for God in peace
and joy.

When God showed me the vision of Jesus dying on the
cross, I saw His blood pouring out like the blood of a slaugh-
tered animal. I saw the loincloth they used to cover Him, and
it was soaked in red blood. I saw blood flowing down His legs.
I saw it dripping from His feet. How much blood He must
have shed! When He finally breathed His last breath, I saw
angels coming and going, picking up the blood and taking it
to God.

I said to one of them, "What are you doing?"

The angel answered, "We're taking this to heaven. It's a
sacrifice to God for the sins of the world." It took what looked
like thousands of angels to carry His blood back to heaven.
Our blessed Lord Himself, the One who was crucified, would,
as our Great High Priest, apply the precious blood on the
mercy seat there. I saw my blessed Lord sprinkle the blood
He shed on earth as a sin offering for me—and for every other
person who would believe in Him.

Again, the tabernacle was only a shadow of the spiritual reality, but Jesus has gone into the Holy of Holies in heaven, the *true* Holy of Holies, into the very presence of God. He has taken with Him *"better sacrifices"* (Hebrews 9:23)—His own atoning blood and Himself as the ultimate sacrifice. All the Old Testament sacrifices and offerings find their fulfillment and completion in Him.

Jesus has gone into God's presence on behalf of His people just as the high priest of old did for the Hebrew people. This is where the Lord is now, where He *"always lives to make intercession for* [us]" (Hebrews 7:25). He effectively deals with the power of sin in our lives when we commit ourselves fully to Him. His atoning blood satisfies the justice of God, and through His blood we obtain forgiveness.

There is a great difference between Jesus the Great High Priest and the high priests who served under the old covenant. Israel's high priest could not stay in the Holy of Holies. After the brief sacrificial ritual, he had to leave that holy place. As he left, the veil separating the Holy of Holies from the rest of the tabernacle fell behind him again, shutting him out for another year.

Yet when Jesus sacrificed Himself on the cross, the Bible says that the curtain in the temple was ripped from top to bottom. (See Matthew 27:51.) This signified that the old covenant had been done away with and the new covenant through Jesus Christ had come into being.

This comparison becomes more real and meaningful with a careful study of the high priestly ministry of Christ. Hebrews 7–9 discusses various aspects of the high priest's ministry and culminates with an explanation of Jesus entering heaven as the High Priest and delivering the blood of the sacrifice—the sacrifice of Himself—before the heavenly mercy seat. It is a beautiful picture of the completed work of Christ. When I saw Jesus enter into heaven's Most Holy Place in the vision, He did not falter or hesitate. He marched boldly to heaven's altar and poured out His blood. It was a decisive and final action.

The eternal price has been paid. The Lamb that was slain from the foundation of the world has once and for all taken away the sins of the world. Now He stands as the faithful and merciful High Priest, His sacrificial work completed. The blood has been delivered, and mankind can be redeemed. *"He shall see the labor of His soul, and be satisfied. By His knowledge My righteous Servant shall justify many, for He shall bear their iniquities"* (Isaiah 53:11).

Our High Priest is fully qualified to fulfill His roles as Mediator and Intercessor. He has opened a *"new and living way"* (Hebrews 10:20) by which each of us can approach God. Because of His sacrifice, we are now sons and daughters of the heavenly Father. We can indeed come boldly into God's presence with great confidence, assured of His grace. (See Hebrews 4:16.) The benefits of His intercessory work are now open to us. We can experience the "sweet hour of prayer," because He

> ...bids me at my Father's throne
> Make all my wants and wishes known.[1]

It is a great comfort to realize that we have a High Priest who represents us before the throne of God. This is especially true since we have an *"accuser"* (Revelation 12:10) who constantly opposes us and brings charges against us before the Father. Christ is our Advocate in God's presence.

> *Therefore, in all things He had to be made like His brethren, that He might be a merciful and faithful High Priest in things pertaining to God, to make propitiation for the sins of the people....Therefore, holy brethren, partakers of the heavenly calling, consider the Apostle and High Priest of our confession, Christ Jesus, who was faithful to Him who appointed Him, as Moses also was faithful in all His house.*
>
> (Hebrews 2:17; 3:1–2)

Because Christ is the *"Faithful and True"* (Revelation 19:11), I can trust Him. Because He is victorious, He can help me escape the tempter's snare. Because He earnestly calls me to seek His face, I can confidently open my heart to Him. This High Priest—because of His accomplishments through the blood—assures me of deliverance, freedom, forgiveness, and power.

THE NEW COVENANT PEOPLE OF GOD

Through the new covenant, God has gained for Himself a new covenant people. There is no longer any distinction between Jew or Gentile for those who have believed in the atoning work of Christ on their behalf. Instead, a new people of God has been created. Paul wrote, *"There is neither Greek nor Jew, circumcised nor uncircumcised, barbarian, Scythian, slave nor free, but Christ is all and in all"* (Colossians 3:11), and *"For He Himself is our peace, who has made both one, and has broken down the middle wall of separation"* (Ephesians 2:14).

The Bible indicates that God takes very seriously the relationship He has with the church. The church was not an afterthought in His mind, nor was it a creation of man. It was part of the divine initiative, and it depended on the precious blood of Jesus Christ for its genesis.

Nowhere is this truth clearer than in the exhortation of Paul to the Ephesian believers in Acts 20:28:

Therefore take heed to yourselves and to all the flock, among which the Holy Spirit has made you overseers, to shepherd the church of God which He purchased with His own blood.

Whatever criticisms the world has about the church, and no matter how neglectful so-called Christians may become in their devotion to it, this fact remains: The church originated in the mind of God and was purchased with the precious blood of the Savior. No one can fully understand the nature of the church without taking into consideration the blood of the Lamb that bought it.

UNDERSTANDING THE SPIRITUAL FAMILY OF GOD

Today, we use the word *church* in many different ways. It distinguishes religious people from nonreligious; it describes denominations (Methodist, Church of God, Baptist, and so on); it refers to a building where people gather to worship; it sometimes means something universal and sometimes something local. Because we use these various definitions for the church, its true meaning is often obscured.

The church is the spiritual family of God. It is the Christian fellowship bought by the blood of the Lamb slain from the foundation of the world. It had its beginning in the counsels of eternity and its literal genesis when Jesus gathered

His disciples around Him, taught them, and commissioned them to do His work in the world. It flamed into visible existence on the Day of Pentecost. (See Acts 2.)

The word *church* appears numerous times in the New Testament. In the great majority of cases, it refers to a local body of believers. In other cases, it refers to the church in general, sometimes called the universal church. We use that term today to signify the body of Christ that transcends time and reaches across the centuries, including all people, living and dead, who have trusted in Christ and have become part of the family of God, bought with the blood of the Lamb.

The church is both a divine institution and a human one. It is divine because Jesus said, *"I will build My church, and the gates of Hades shall not prevail against it"* (Matthew 16:18). It is also human because Paul reminded us, as he was discussing the building of the church, that *"we are God's fellow workers"* (1 Corinthians 3:9). Wherever the Holy Spirit unites believers to Christ and to other believers, the church exists.

The church is called to fulfill the work that the Lord of the church has given it to do. It is a place where the gospel is proclaimed, where God is worshiped, where the Spirit directs the conduct of the worshipers, where baptism and the Lord's Supper are practiced, and where people are *"endeavoring to keep the unity of the Spirit in the bond of peace"* (Ephesians 4:3).

THE REVELATION OF
THE CHURCH

The revelation of the nature of the church in the New Testament is multifaceted. Only by considering the names and metaphors that the Word uses to identify it can we understand the mystery and beauty of God's plan for the church as the new covenant people of God.

THE CHURCH AS BRIDE

First, the church is revealed as the bride of Christ. This depiction fulfills the Old Testament view of the people of God as espoused to Jehovah. The imagery of the bride is a revelation of the loving and special relationship that exists between Christ and the church. A wonderfully clear statement of this relationship appears in Ephesians 5:25: *"Husbands, love your wives, just as Christ also loved the church and gave Himself for her."*

In eastern lands during Bible times (and even in some places today), it was customary for the groom to pay a price to the family of the bride for the privilege of marrying her. The wonderful and awesome truth revealed here is that Christ paid the price for His bride, the church, and the price was His own precious blood.

THE CHURCH AS CHRIST'S BODY

Perhaps one of the most familiar pictures of the church in the New Testament is the body of Christ. *"He is the head of the body, the church"* (Colossians 1:18). Paul frequently used this image, as he did in Ephesians 1:22–23: *"He put all things under His feet, and gave Him to be head over all things to the church, which is His body, the fullness of Him who fills all in all."* Once more, in 1 Corinthians 12:12, we read, *"For as the body is one and has many members, but all the members of that one body, being many, are one body, so also is Christ."*

This analogy assures us that our Head provides wisdom and direction as the body carries out His work. This is the ideal relationship that should always exist between the One who paid the blood-price and the church He purchased. Christ's blood gives life to His body.

Some people object to the idea of the "body" also being the "bride," asking how one can also be the other. This objection dissolves when we remember that, in God's view, husband and wife are *"one flesh"* (Matthew 19:5). The depiction of the church as a bride conveys a message of love; its depiction as a body conveys a message of life.

THE CHURCH AS BRANCHES, FLOCK, LIVING STONES

The New Testament is rich with other images of the church, including the following: He is the vine, and we are the branches (John 15:5). He is the shepherd, and we are the flock. (See, for example, John 10:16.) He is the foundation, and we are the building blocks. (See, for example, 1 Peter 2:4–5.)

All these images have one thing in common: They are living things. In the instance of an inanimate image—stones—Peter labeled them *"living stones"* (v. 5), underlining the truth that the church is a living organism.

The new covenant is about new life—spiritual life through the precious blood of Christ.

6

THE POWER OF THE BLOODLINE

"When I see the blood, I will pass over you."
—Exodus 12:13

Our salvation in Christ includes the protective covering of His precious blood. When we pray for protection in this way, we are affirming that we believe Jesus provided a covering for ourselves and our families through the Atonement. The angels go to us immediately to seal and protect us. Through the blood covenant, we have this hedge of protection, which I call the "bloodline."

THE BLOODLINE DESIGNATES THE FAMILY OF GOD

Let's begin by looking at the nature of the bloodline. First, it is a defining line. Spiritually speaking, the blood of Jesus forms a line of demarcation between believers and those who are separated and alienated from God. When the heavenly Father sees the blood of Jesus applied to our hearts, that is a signal to all of heaven that we are His own. Only the blood of Christ saves the believer from separation from God.

Until you cross the bloodline, you have no hope of salvation. When you put your faith in the atoning blood of Jesus, however, you are protected by the blood.

THE BLOODLINE DIVIDES

The cross has great power to unite people to God and each other, but it also can cause a significant division in human relations. The relationship between the redeemed and the Redeemer is greater than any human relationship, even one of flesh and blood. When one person is a believer and another is not, the spiritual division between them is vast. Sometimes, this division can cause conflicts, even in one's family. Jesus said,

Do not think that I came to bring peace on earth. I did not come to bring peace but a sword. For I have come to "set a man against his father, a daughter against her mother, and a daughter-in-law against her mother-in-law"; and "a man's enemies will be those of his own household." He who loves father or mother more than Me is not worthy of Me. And he who loves son or daughter more than Me is not worthy of Me.

(Matthew 10:34–37)

Jesus also told of the day when all of mankind—every man, woman and child who has ever lived—will experience the division established by the blood of Jesus Christ.

When the Son of Man comes in His glory, and all the holy angels with Him, then He will sit on the throne of His glory. All the nations will be gathered before Him, and He will separate them one from another, as a shepherd divides his sheep from the goats.

(Matthew 25:31–32)

The bloodline will be the difference on that day!

An example of this division can be seen in the story of the Israelites in Egypt, which we began to look at in an earlier chapter. On nine occasions, Moses took God's demands to Pharaoh, telling him to let the Israelites journey into the wilderness to worship. Each time Pharaoh refused, and each time a plague was sent upon Egypt. Both the Egyptians and the Israelites suffered the effects of the first three plagues. But when it was time for the fourth plague, the Lord instructed Moses to tell Pharaoh,

> *In that day I will set apart the land of Goshen, in which My people dwell…in order that you may know that I am the* Lord *in the midst of the land. I will make a difference between My people and your people.*
> (Exodus 8:22–23)

THE BLOODLINE AS PROTECTION

The bloodline is also a sign of protection. The precious blood of Christ is set forever before the eyes of God, and we are safe as long as we are under it. The tenth and final plague in Egypt was the death of the firstborn in every house. The horror of that particular evening must have been overwhelming. This is the Bible's account of it:

> *And it came to pass at midnight that the* Lord *struck all the firstborn in the land of Egypt, from the firstborn of Pharaoh who sat on his throne to the firstborn of the captive who was in the dungeon, and all the firstborn of livestock. So Pharaoh rose in the night, he, all his servants, and all the Egyptians; and there was*

*a great cry in Egypt, for there was not a house where
there was not one dead.*   (Exodus 12:29–30)

The Israelite families, however, were protected. God, who
is merciful and full of compassion, provided a way for His
people to be shielded from this terrible plague; it was through
the shedding of blood in the observance of the first Passover.
We are told that *"just as the LORD had commanded Moses and
Aaron, so they did"* (v. 28). This statement is in regard to the
instruction to kill the Passover lamb, eat the Passover meal,
and, especially, to spread the blood of the lamb on the doorposts and lintels of their homes.

The Lord told the Israelites that the death angel would
pass through Egypt, but that

> *the blood shall be a sign for you on the houses where
> you are. And when I see the blood, I will pass over
> you; and the plague shall not be on you to destroy you
> when I strike the land of Egypt.*   (Exodus 12:13)

The blood would separate them from the disobedient
Egyptians in God's sight.

The clear meaning to the Israelites was this: "Do not
cross the bloodline or you will not be protected." Likewise,
God's instructions to the death angel must have been, "Do not
cross the bloodline!" The Israelites believed God and placed

the blood of the Passover lamb between themselves and the destroying angel.

The Passover was the first feast unto the Lord that God commanded the nation of Israel to keep. (See Exodus 12:13–20.) He told them to observe this feast perpetually to remember the deliverance He was about to grant them. Today, we know that Christ, our Passover, was sacrificed for us. (See 1 Corinthians 5:7.) More powerful than the power of death and evil is the blood of the Lamb of God!

When I began to seek the Lord about the blood of Christ, He prompted me to pray and dedicate everything around me to the Father, Son, and Holy Spirit, through the blood of the Lamb. He said that I would have visions of angels coming from heaven, laden with crosses. As I dedicated churches, buildings, houses, children, and other things to the Lord, I saw these angels. Also, it was as if the blood was on the ground in the form of a circle or a line of the blood of the Lamb, and the demons could not cross over it. A liberating revelation came to me when God revealed to me the truth about the bloodline.

In the Israelites' old covenant with God, the people were explicitly promised that if they kept the law, God would honor and prosper them. (See Deuteronomy 28.) If they failed to keep the law, however, they would incur the punishment of God. Now we have a new and better covenant:

*The days are coming, says the LORD, when I will make
a new covenant...not according to the covenant that
I made with their fathers in the day that I took them
by the hand to lead them out of the land of Egypt, My
covenant which they broke, though I was a husband
to them, says the LORD. But this is the covenant that
I will make...: I will put My law in their minds, and
write it on their hearts; and I will be their God, and
they shall be My people.* (Jeremiah 31:31–33)

When God sees the blood applied to your life, He will
defend and protect you. The bloodline is a line of defense
around believers who have trusted in Him. Just as the bloodline protected the Israelites in Egypt, so Christ's bloodline
will protect you and keep you safe. If God Himself had great
respect for the blood marking the doors of His obedient
people, how much more will Satan have to respect the bloodline marking the children of God when he sees the blood of
God's own Son applied to their hearts!

THE BLOODLINE DELIVERS

God's instructions for the partaking of the first Passover
meal were specific: *"Thus you shall eat it: with a belt on your
waist, your sandals on your feet, and your staff in your hand. So
you shall eat it in haste. It is the LORD's Passover"* (Exodus 12:11).

WHEN GOD SEES THE BLOOD
APPLIED TO YOUR LIFE, HE WILL
DEFEND AND PROTECT YOU.
THE BLOODLINE IS A LINE OF
DEFENSE AROUND BELIEVERS
WHO HAVE TRUSTED IN HIM.
JUST AS THE BLOODLINE
PROTECTED THE ISRAELITES IN
EGYPT, SO CHRIST'S BLOODLINE
WILL PROTECT YOU AND
KEEP YOU SAFE.

God had deliverance planned for His people, and He intended to do it quickly. While the blood on the doorways protected those within the Israelites' houses, they ate the roasted flesh of the lamb from which the blood had come. They ate it as though they would soon be taking a long journey. God intended the deliverance of Israel to be as fast as the hand of death traveling through Egypt.

In the homes of the Israelites that evening, I believe there was a sense of peace, protection, and satisfaction. The people had consumed a hearty meal, and they sat in anticipation with their shoes on their feet and their garments on their backs. Within the confines of their blood-streaked doors, they awaited Moses's command to move out.

Meanwhile, in the homes of the Egyptians, those who had prepared to settle in for an evening of rest suddenly found that death had entered their homes through unguarded doors. The Bible tells us what happened next:

> *So Pharaoh rose in the night, he, all his servants, and all the Egyptians; and there was a great cry in Egypt, for there was not a house where there was not one dead. Then he called for Moses and Aaron by night, and said, "Rise, go out from among my people, both you and the children of Israel. And go, serve the LORD as you have said. Also take your flocks and your herds, as you have said, and be gone; and bless me also." And*

> *the Egyptians urged the people, that they might send*
> *them out of the land in haste. For they said, "We shall*
> *all be dead."*   (Exodus 12:30–33)

The bloodline made the difference between life and death. The presence of the blood of the Passover lambs on the doorways of the Hebrews provided their deliverance. Without the blood, Israel would have mourned as deeply for her firstborn as Egypt did. Without the blood, Israel would have been journeying to burial tombs instead of to the Promised Land.

Through the blood of Jesus Christ, God's Passover Lamb, we can be delivered from sin and harm today. People who have been enslaved by physical, emotional, and mental lusts to the point that they have no recourse in the world have applied the precious blood of the Lamb to their hearts and been delivered, and an indescribable freedom has overtaken them.

The cross has become our doorway into the divinely protected place of deliverance and peace. I invite you to receive Christ into your heart and find refuge behind His bloodline today.

PLEADING THE BLOOD

I want to conclude this chapter with an explanation of what it means to "plead the blood." God has shown me the importance of the cross and the blood covenant with its accompanying protection. "Pleading the blood of Jesus" is more than just a catchphrase. It is, in a sense, a legal term. It means to invoke what Christ has done on the cross over a particular situation or person. A blood covering is provided through faith in God, prayer, and belief in the covenant of God. I have learned that when we are praying for people, and God impresses upon us to cover people with the blood, we should say, "I cover you with the blood of Jesus, the covenant of God!"

We should never be ashamed of the blood of the Lamb. When we say that we cover others with the precious blood of Jesus Christ, this means that we claim the blood that He shed, which enabled us to enter into the new covenant with God. It means that Almighty God will look down from heaven and watch over us and protect us. It means that we can pray over our children and cover them with the covenant blood of Jesus Christ. Demons tremble at the name of Jesus, and they flee at the blood of the Lamb.

Pleading the blood gives us bold and confident access to God's power and providence. As the Scripture says, we can have *"boldness to enter the Holiest by the blood of Jesus, by a new and living way which He consecrated for us, through...His flesh"* (Hebrews 10:19–20).

For example, we can plead the blood for ourselves when the devil tries to torment us with the memory of past sins that have already been forgiven. Doing this reminds us and the devil that God has forgotten our sins because of Christ's sacrifice and His blood. The Word of God says, *"They overcame him by the blood of the Lamb and by the word of their testimony"* (Revelation 12:11). I believe that *"the word of* [our] *testimony"* simply means believing in the efficacy of the blood.

A believer who pleads the blood in a time of dire circumstance or attack by the enemy is calling on the power and authority of Christ's blood. When we plead the blood, we acknowledge and testify to the overcoming power of the sacrifice of Jesus on our behalf. To defeat the devil, you need to stand on the blood and proclaim its power! In the next few chapters, we will look at specific applications of the power of the blood in our lives.

7

SALVATION THROUGH THE BLOOD

"Much more then, having now been justified
by His blood, we shall be saved
from wrath through Him."
—Romans 5:9

Salvation is the first application of the blood of Christ to our lives. Although we've talked about this theme in various ways throughout this book, it deserves an even closer look because of its enormous importance.

Of all the revelations that God has given to me, none has impacted me in a greater way than the knowledge that the core of true faith, regardless of any disagreements Christians may have over denominational doctrines, is the fact that salvation comes only through the blood of Jesus Christ. In fact, in the New Testament, the blood of Christ is linked directly to the saving significance of Jesus's death twenty-five times.

I believe that the first encounter a person has with the blood of Jesus, when it is applied to his or her heart by faith, is by far the most meaningful and life-altering experience that person will ever have. Every born-again believer has this encounter with the blood of Jesus in a spiritual, yet very real, sense when he or she repents and believes God for justification through Christ. Nothing on earth can compare with the sense of cleansing and refreshing that comes when Jesus washes away every sin and transgression.

When Jesus's blood is applied to a person's life, it renders him spotless before God. What rejoicing takes place in the life of one who has been born again! At first glance, it may seem as if the new believer is the same person, having all his former physical features and nature. Yet, those natural features often somehow seem renewed. A sense of newness surrounds the newly born child of God. He or she often takes on a beauty that is unmistakable to the observer.

Yet the internal transformation that takes place at the time of the new birth defies physical description and stands as one of the most mysterious events in Christian experience. The Bible tells us, *"Therefore, if anyone is in Christ, he is a new creation; old things have passed away; behold, all things have become new"* (2 Corinthians 5:17).

The most drastic changes take place in the heart, soul, and mind. The guilt that has characterized the individual for so long is lifted. Guilt is one of the most troublesome mental stresses that a person can suffer. It weighs heavily on the conscience and constantly nags at the heart and mind like an ulcer.

Guilt has the ability to awaken us out of a peaceful sleep to torment us with blazing accusations. It builds walls between us and our neighbors. It distorts our conversations with anxiety and seems to loom over our shoulders during every waking moment. Guilt is one of Satan's most versatile tools of destruction.

Yet where the blood of Jesus flows, all guilt can be washed away. When real salvation comes, real guilt is removed. Without guilt, the heart is free to soar as the heart of Adam did when he walked with God in the cool of the day. (See Genesis 3:8.) Without guilt, the mind is free to contemplate the joys of knowing the God of forgiveness in a way it had never before imagined.

Let's look at the many ways that the blood of Jesus provides for our salvation.

THE BLOOD PROVIDES REDEMPTION

First, it is by the blood that we are redeemed from sin. Outside the church, one of the only places the term *redemption* is heard is in the pawnshop. A customer comes in and leaves something of value—his watch, for instance—for which the pawnbroker pays him a certain amount of money. If the man wishes to reclaim his watch, he must return and pay the pawnbroker the amount he had received from him plus an additional fee. This reclaiming of his property by payment is called "redemption."

Our souls were in pawn, so to speak, but the blood of Jesus paid the redemption price that nothing else was sufficient to pay. The blood of Jesus Christ alone has the power to liberate us from the prison of sin. It can cleanse the vilest transgressors and make them pure and whole. The apostle Peter reminded us that we were not redeemed with corruptible, or temporary, things but with the precious blood of Jesus:

You were not redeemed with corruptible things, like silver or gold, from your aimless conduct received by tradition from your fathers, but with the precious blood of Christ, as of a lamb without blemish and without spot. He indeed was foreordained before the foundation of the world, but was manifest in these last times for you who through Him believe in God, who raised Him from the dead and gave Him glory, so that your faith and hope are in God.   (1 Peter 1:18–21)

The Scripture plainly says that *"without shedding of blood there is no remission* [forgiveness]*"* (Hebrews 9:22). Jesus affirmed, *"For this is My blood of the new covenant, which is shed for many for the remission of sins"* (Matthew 26:28). Ephesians 1:7 and Colossians 1:14 both tell us that in Christ *"we have redemption through His blood, the forgiveness of sins."*

Again, only Jesus's blood can redeem us. Money is a powerful commodity, but there is not enough money in the world to redeem a single sinner. Forgiveness is not cheap; it cost God the life of His Son. When Jesus sacrificed His life, it hurt Him deeply. There was agonizing pain involved. He knew that He had to carry the weight of the whole world on His shoulders, but He was willing to do it in order to save us from eternal separation from God. The blood of Christ is the bedrock of our faith and lives.

It was a glorious revelation to me to understand that God gives us His life through the blood of Jesus. We must depend on the blood to do what God says it will do. When we do, we will not try to rely on our own works or performance, which cannot save us. If you believe that you can perform well enough or be good enough to merit God's approval without the blood of Jesus, you are deceived. We do not obtain salvation through works or good deeds. We gain salvation through faith in the blood of Jesus and by our verbal affirmation that we want Jesus to be the Lord and King over our lives. (See Romans 10:9.)

As we saw earlier, in the Old Testament, a curtain or veil separated the priest—the one who offered the blood on the altar—and the person seeking forgiveness and cleansing. In a spiritual sense, the curtain that separates us from God is the reality of sin in our lives. Sin has an undeniable power in our fleshly nature. This veil of "sinful flesh" can be removed from us only when sin is taken away from us. We cannot take away the veil in our own strength. We cannot remove sin from our flesh by doing good deeds or by any of our own efforts. But there is hope: The Lamb of God has removed the veil.

> *For what the law could not do in that it was weak through the flesh, God did by sending His own Son in the likeness of sinful flesh, on account of sin: He condemned sin in the flesh, that the righteous requirement of the law might be fulfilled in us who do not walk according to the flesh but according to the Spirit.*
>
> (Romans 8:3–4)

This means that when Jesus came to earth as a human being, He removed the veil by offering up His body as our Substitute, thus canceling the power of sinful flesh within us.

"A new and living way...He consecrated for us, through the veil, that is, His flesh [body]" (Hebrew 10:20). Now it is a glorious privilege for us to enter into the heavenly Holy of Holies and dwell there in the presence of God. (See verse 22.) All this is possible because the Lamb of God shed His blood for us.

THE BLOOD PROVIDES ATONEMENT

The various animals and offerings given for atonement in the Old Testament taught us two things. First, nothing man could do could completely atone, once and for all, for the sins of mankind. Second, the all-inclusive nature of the various sacrifices of atonement prefigured the completeness of the shedding of Christ's blood on the cross. Also, just as atonement was limited to the people of God who abided by a covenant with Him, so redemption and atonement today are limited to those who accept Jesus by faith in His shed blood.

Jesus Christ entered into the very throne room of His Father, carrying His own precious blood. Today His blood calls to us some 3,500 years after the first Day of Atonement, urging us, "Enter in. Do not worship from afar! You have standing before God!"

The blood of Jesus was the price paid to free us from the prison of sin. Jesus's atonement covers *all* your sins: those that are intentional and those that are unintentional; those that are abhorrent and those that appear trivial.

THE BLOOD OF JESUS
PROVIDES JUSTIFICATION

Again, the blood of Jesus does not just cover our sins, but it completely pays for them, fulfilling the righteous requirements of God.

> *Being justified freely by His grace through the redemption that is in Christ Jesus, whom God set forth as a propitiation by His blood, through faith, to demonstrate His righteousness, because in His forbearance God had passed over the sins that were previously committed.* (Romans 3:24–25)

The Bible clearly states that we are justified by His blood. This means that we are made to be as if we had *never* sinned.

> *God demonstrates His own love toward us, in that while we were still sinners, Christ died for us. Much more then, having now been justified by His blood, we shall be saved from wrath through Him.*
> (Romans 5:8–9)

One of the results of justification is that we have peace with God, and this enables us to experience a reconciled relationship to Him. "*In Christ Jesus you who were once far off have been brought near by the blood of Christ*" (Ephesians 2:13). The blood of Christ saves us from the wrath of God. (See

Romans 5:9.) It also enables us to overcome the power of our accuser, Satan. (See Revelation 12:11.) Because of the blood of Christ, Satan is powerless to convict us of sin.

THE BLOOD PROVIDES COMPLETE FORGIVENESS

When the Word of God says, "*Without shedding of blood there is no remission*" (Hebrews 9:22), the word "*remission*" is not the word we use when we talk about a cancer being in remission. If cancer is in remission, then it is possible for it to come back. The word in this passage is "a dismissal, release."[1] It means to totally annihilate as if it had never existed. It can never come back. The Spirit of God assures us that sins once forgiven can never be held against us again. Our sins are totally removed, and God does not remember them any longer. When we ask God to forgive our sins, the blood of Jesus removes them totally.

David spoke of this idea when he said, "*As far as the east is from the west, so far has He removed our transgressions from us*" (Psalm 103:12). Note the geographical truth of David's statement. Before man discovered that the earth is round, God obviously knew the shape of the planet, and He revealed through David a wondrous aspect of salvation: just how far God removes our sins from us. For example, if you were to board an airplane and begin flying north, at a certain point, you would begin going south again. If you travel far enough south, you will start to go north again. Yet east and west never meet. You can board an airplane and travel east or west to infinity.

David said that's how far God has removed our sins from us. The blood of Jesus Christ not only washes away our sins, but it also eradicates sin from us and leaves our souls spotless, as only He can make them.

THE BLOOD PROVIDES CLEANSING

The blood of Jesus also *"cleanses us from all sin"* (1 John 1:7). Often, in my visions from God, I have seen images of sin hanging like heavy millstones around the necks of individuals. These desolate images are graphic illustrations of the spiritual state of all who have not confessed and believed in Jesus Christ for forgiveness.

When we accept Him, however, the precious blood of the Lamb of God purifies us from all the transgressions we have ever committed. *"To Him who loved us and washed us from our sins in His own blood"* (Revelation 1:5). The cross transforms us forever. I know that I am totally clean and restored.

There is nothing quite like the power and confidence you feel when you know you are innocent. If you know your cause is just and that you are in the right, then you can face anyone who might try to condemn you. We are not innocent in ourselves because of the sins we have committed. Therefore, we are powerless to defend ourselves against God's judgment. However, the blood of Christ changes everything. Hebrews 13:12 tells us that we are sanctified through the blood of Jesus. This means we are made holy before God.

Although similar in nature, purification and reconciliation are two separate actions. Through the blood of Christ, a believer who receives the Lord Jesus Christ into his heart is purified from sin and guilt, which enables him to be reconciled to God at the same time.

This is what we desperately need: the sin-forgiving, guilt-removing, heart-cleansing, conscience-purifying blood of Jesus. Wash in it, and you will be *whiter than snow* (Psalm 51:7).

> *How much more shall the blood of Christ, who through the eternal Spirit offered Himself without spot to God, cleanse your conscience from dead works to serve the living God?* (Hebrews 9:14)

I am so grateful for the blood of Jesus. Many times in services, I see the walls covered in red. I see the front of the altar covered in red. As people come up to give their lives to God, I see them washed and cleansed. They say, "Oh, I feel so clean. I feel like I've been washed in the river of life." Many times, I have also seen demons release their control of the people they have possessed and then flee.

MEDICINE SOMETIMES HAS
IMPRESSIVE POWER TO HEAL THE
SICK, BUT ONLY THE
BLOOD OF JESUS CHRIST CAN
RAISE THE DEAD. ANY FOOL WITH
A GUN CAN TAKE A LIFE,
BUT ONLY THE BLOOD OF JESUS
CAN BRING LIFE BACK. THROUGH
JESUS'S BLOOD, THOSE WHO
BELIEVE IN HIM WILL SURVIVE
DEATH ITSELF; THEY WILL LIVE
ETERNALLY WITH GOD!

Some time ago, I was in Trinidad preaching the gospel. I strongly emphasized the power of the blood of Jesus to save people from their sins. When I gave the altar invitation, hundreds of people—most of them Muslims—came forward to receive the Lord Jesus Christ as Savior.

THE BLOOD PROVIDES RESURRECTION AND ETERNAL LIFE

The blood of Jesus also has the power of resurrection. Just as a body emptied of blood becomes a corpse, so faith devoid of the cleansing blood of Jesus is dead faith. Or it is misplaced faith in a dead cause.

Medicine sometimes has impressive power to heal the sick, but only the blood of Jesus Christ can raise the dead. Any fool with a gun can take a life, but only the blood of Jesus can bring life back. Through Jesus's blood, those who believe in Him will survive death itself; they will live eternally with God! Jesus said,

Most assuredly, I say to you, he who believes in Me has everlasting life. I am the bread of life. Your fathers ate the manna in the wilderness, and are dead. This is the bread which comes down from heaven, that one may eat of it and not die. I am the living bread which came down from heaven. If anyone eats of this bread, he will live forever; and the bread that I shall give is

> *My flesh, which I shall give for the life of the world.*
> (John 6:47–51)

The age-old hunger in the human heart is to live forever. We want to know that we will still exist after we die. Jesus has provided for our hunger to be filled. All major religions teach some form of existence after death, but only Christianity can say that its founder *demonstrated* life after death.

> *Inasmuch then as the children have partaken of flesh and blood, He Himself likewise shared in the same, that through death He might destroy him who had the power of death, that is, the devil, and release those who through fear of death were all their lifetime subject to bondage.*   (Hebrews 2:14–15)

Jesus came to give abundant life on earth (see John 10:10), but He also came to give eternal life forever: *"I am the resurrection and the life. He who believes in Me, though he may die, he shall live. And whoever lives and believes in Me shall never die"* (John 11:25–26). Since life is in the blood, it is through His blood that we will live after death. I believe the Bible tells us that Jesus Himself was resurrected *by His own blood:*

> *Now may the God of peace who brought up our Lord Jesus from the dead, that great Shepherd of the sheep, through the blood of the everlasting covenant, make*

*you complete in every good work to do His will, work-
ing in you what is well pleasing in His sight.*

(Hebrews 13:20–21)

Because Jesus lives, believers will also survive the deaths
of their bodies through the precious blood of the Lamb. One
day, we will join the redeemed saints in heaven, along with
the cherubim and the twenty-four elders (see Revelation 5:11),
and we will sing, *"Worthy is the Lamb who was slain to receive
power and riches and wisdom, and strength and honor and glory
and blessing!"* (v. 12).

THE GREATEST SACRIFICE

The story is told of two children in the same family who
were born with a rare blood type and had to be treated with
extreme care by physicians. The little boy, who was only three
years old, began to experience some grave health problems.
The boy needed a blood transfusion, and his five-year-old sister
was the only possible blood donor to be found. Carefully, the
parents and doctors tried to explain the situation to the little
girl: Her brother needed blood, and she was the only one who
could give it to him.

The girl thought it over very carefully and finally con-
sented for the doctors to take her blood and give it to her
brother. As she lay on a table, a needle was inserted into her
arm. She watched intently as her blood flowed into the plastic

container that would be used to transfer it to her brother. When the procedure was finished, the nurse took the needle from her arm and told her, "It's all over."

Perplexed, the little girl asked, "But when do I die?" She had misunderstood what the procedure would mean for her, yet she willingly gave her blood, thinking it meant her own death.

Such a tender and loving spirit is rare today. Only a few of us would gladly give up our lives for our loved ones if it were necessary. Only one Person could atone for our sins by shedding His blood, and Jesus willingly and lovingly gave His body and blood that you and I might be saved. No one else was worthy. No one else could have made the sacrifice and paid the price.

CHRIST IN US

From the beginning of Genesis to the end of Revelation, God reveals that He wants a people who will praise and love Him. He knew that no one could keep the Law that was given through Moses, so He sent His own Son to redeem us and give us His Spirit. As we repent and confess our sins to the Lord, and as we give our lives to Him, He does something wonderful—He comes to dwell within us, and our fellowship with our heavenly Father is restored.

I urge you to accept Jesus and His great sacrifice for you. If you do not know Jesus, read the Bible and learn about Him. Understand who He really is. The Bible is the true Word of God, and it says you must be born anew into God's kingdom: *"Jesus answered and said to* [Nicodemus], *'Most assuredly, I say to you, unless one is born again, he cannot see the kingdom of God'"* (John 3:3).

Your sins can be washed away through the atonement Jesus accomplished by shedding His blood on the cross. Even if you think you are the worst person in the world, you can turn to Jesus for complete forgiveness. You can pray, "Jesus, I believe You're the Son of God and my Savior. I believe You died on the cross and rose again so that I can have new life in You. I ask You to wash away my sins through Your cleansing blood and make me clean. Fill me with Your Holy Spirit so that I can now live for You. I commit my life to loving and serving You. Amen."

If you prayed that prayer sincerely from your heart, God will be faithful to forgive you and cleanse you completely. He will give you the gift of His Holy Spirit, who will live within you and enable you to obey and serve God. You will become a part of God's own family, and His angels will watch over you.

One day, the very Person who shed His blood for us will be our Judge. The Scripture says, *"It is appointed unto men once to die, but after this the judgment"* (Hebrews 9:27). It would

DO YOU LONG TO BE FREE
FROM THE BONDS THAT KEEP
YOU FROM ENJOYING LIFE AT
ITS BEST? JESUS SHED HIS
BLOOD SO THAT YOU CAN FIND
FORGIVENESS AND PEACE.
BELIEVE IN THE SIN-ATONING
BLOOD OF JESUS. IT IS GREATER
THAN ALL YOUR SIN. BELIEVE
THAT HE DIED FOR *YOU* AND ROSE
FROM THE DEAD TO FORGIVE *YOU*
OF YOUR SINS.

be well for us to keep the memory of His sacrifice fresh in our hearts at all times and to make a heartfelt commitment to Him. I urge you to do it now, for you do not know at what hour you will face Him as your Judge.

TRUST IN THE BLOOD

You can never make atonement for your past sins, nor can you, by personal obedience, secure a title to the inheritance of glory. Yet Jesus is willing to take away all your sins and give you an inheritance in His glorious kingdom if you will only consent to entrust Him alone with your salvation.

Are you a child of God? Do you know the Lord Jesus Christ as your Savior? Do you struggle with sin in your life? Do you long to be free from the bonds that keep you from enjoying life at its best? Jesus shed His blood so that you can find forgiveness and peace. Believe in the sin-atoning blood of Jesus. It is greater than all your sin. Believe that He died for *you* and rose from the dead to forgive *you* of your sins.

The blood of the Lamb is applied to your heart by faith. The Scripture says, *"By faith he kept the Passover and the sprinkling of blood, lest he who destroyed the firstborn should touch them"* (Hebrews 11:28). Trust in Jesus, your High Priest, to sprinkle your heart with His atoning blood.

His blood is also applied to your heart as you humble yourself before God and seek Him. In this often-quoted prayer for forgiveness, David acknowledged this truth:

You do not desire sacrifice, or else I would give it; You do not delight in burnt offering. The sacrifices of God are a broken spirit, a broken and a contrite heart; these, O God, You will not despise.

(Psalm 51:16–17)

Spiritually speaking, Jesus's blood is pleading for your soul. As I mentioned earlier, His blood is speaking more loudly on behalf of mercy for you than your sins are crying out against you. Yet the powerful blood of Jesus is of no use to you unless it is applied to your heart and conscience.

If you are already a believer, are you living in the full sense of your pardon and acceptance in Jesus? Do you have a present and assured salvation? If not, have you stopped short of the applied blood? Oh, come to *"the blood of sprinkling"* (Hebrews 12:24). Allow no guilt to remain upon your conscience, but wash daily in the precious blood of Christ, which *"cleanses us from **all** sin"* (1 John 1:7, emphasis added).

What can wash away my sin?
Nothing but the blood of Jesus;
What can make me whole again?
Nothing but the blood of Jesus.

O! precious is the flow
That makes me white as snow;
No other fount I know,
Nothing but the blood of Jesus.[2]

Likewise, another poet has said,
There is a fountain filled with blood
Drawn from Immanuel's veins;
And sinners, plunged beneath that flood,
Lose all their guilty stains.[3]

The precious blood of the Lamb is our hope and comfort. There is no limit to what the blood has accomplished and can accomplish. Jesus's blood assures us of salvation and forgiveness. Again, we can't rely on our own goodness for our hope of forgiveness because we could never be good enough to atone for our sins. But Christ's blood has made perfect provision for us. *"In Him we have redemption through His blood, the forgiveness of sins, according to the riches of His grace"* (Ephesians 1:7). His blood did what nothing or no one else ever could have done.

8

PEACE THROUGH
THE BLOOD

*"The chastisement for our peace
was upon Him."*
—Isaiah 53:5

Peace is another main result of the application of the blood
of Christ to our lives:

It pleased the Father that in Him all the fullness
should dwell, and by Him to **reconcile all things**

*to Himself, by Him, whether things on earth or things in heaven, **having made peace through the blood of His cross.** And you, who once were alienated and enemies in your mind by wicked works, yet now He has reconciled in the body of His flesh through death, to present you holy, and blameless, and above reproach in His sight.*

(Colossians 1:19–22, emphasis added)

When God created the first man, He established a relationship of love and trust between Himself and Adam. This was the beginning of all human relationships with the Creator. God also formed the first woman, Eve, and established a relationship with both of them. Since that time, the lives of all the great believers in the Bible have demonstrated that God desires a personal relationship with human beings. We see this truth played out in the lives of Abraham, Noah, Moses, Peter, Paul, and many others.

Tragically, however, the Creator's deep closeness and unity with humanity was broken when Adam and Eve turned their backs on God and chose rebellion rather than relationship. A wall was created between the heavenly Father and His created offspring. This separation was symbolized by the curtain, or veil, in the tabernacle and temple, which we have discussed.

In my visions, I have often seen what looked like a literal barrier that sin has created between God and man. This barrier represents man's basic hostility toward God. The Scripture tells us, *"The carnal mind is enmity against God; for it is not subject to the law of God, nor indeed can be. So then, those who are in the flesh cannot please God"* (Romans 8:7–8). Yet Christ's blood has the power, through forgiveness, to bring together God and man, and man and man.

PEACE WITH GOD

Colossians 1:20 says that Jesus *"made peace through the blood of His cross."* Jesus's blood has such marvelous power that, through it, we have a *"new and living way"* (Hebrews 10:20) into the presence of God and into peace with God. What does this peace through the blood mean for us?

OUR ENMITY AGAINST GOD IS DISSOLVED

First, we no longer need to be at enmity with God. People are often either hostile to God or trying to ignore Him because their unresolved guilt brings out feelings of self-preservation and causes them to resent Him. They fear punishment, so they run from His presence. Yet Christ has paid the penalty that we deserved, so there's nothing that we have to "protect" ourselves against in God's presence. In fact, the Bible says that we can go boldly into God's presence and ask for help in time of need. (See Hebrews 4:16.)

OUR CLOSE FELLOWSHIP WITH GOD IS RESTORED

Second, the blood has the power to bring us back into deep fellowship with God. We can have intimate communion with Him, just as He intended for us to have. *"In Christ Jesus you who were once far off have been brought near by the blood of Christ"* (Ephesians 2:13). By the effectiveness of Jesus's sacrifice, the sons and daughters of God may receive personal peace and the restitution of their relationship with their heavenly Father.

When we are cleansed by the blood of the cross, God reaches out and pulls us close to Him. You are wanted by Him! He desired you to be His child when you were still in your mother's womb. This was the main reason for the cross—to reconcile us with our heavenly Father. *"We also rejoice in God through our Lord Jesus Christ, through whom we have now received the reconciliation"* (Romans 5:11).

As a child of God, you may be rejected by your family, friends, and others, but you are not—and you never will be—rejected by your heavenly Father. Not only did Christ our High Priest declare you cleansed and forgiven, not only does the Judge of the universe declare you righteous, but He also declares that you are His friend. (See John 15:15.) He is a Friend who will walk and talk with you and who will be with you in times of trouble. When you begin to understand the depths of God's love for you, you will develop a sweet fellowship with Him. Imagine, we can actually be friends—kindred spirits, soul mates—of the Almighty!

GOD'S PEACE GUARDS OUR HEARTS AND MINDS

Third, through the blood of Christ, we experience a peace that keeps us calm and moving forward during difficult times. Jesus told His disciples just before His crucifixion, *"Peace I leave with you, My peace I give to you; not as the world gives do I give to you. Let not your heart be troubled, neither let it be afraid"* (John 14:27). The apostle Paul encouraged the believers with this thought:

> *Be anxious for nothing, but in everything by prayer and supplication, with thanksgiving, let your requests be made known to God; and the peace of God, which surpasses all understanding, will guard your hearts and minds through Christ Jesus.*
>
> (Philippians 4:6–7)

THE LORD'S SUPPER REPRESENTS OUR PEACE WITH GOD

Our peace with God is reflected whenever we partake of the Lord's Supper, and we may use this occasion to deepen our communion with Him. This is because the celebration of the Lord's Supper is a vital part of every Christian's relationship with God. Our observance of this sacrament forever reminds us in a personal way of the price that was paid for our salvation. It is also an act of personal obedience and testimony.

When Jesus inaugurated the Lord's Supper, He gave specific instructions for it:

> *And He took bread, gave thanks and broke it, and gave it to them, saying, "This is My body which is given for you; do this in remembrance of Me." Likewise He also took the cup after supper, saying, "This cup is the new covenant in My blood, which is shed for you."*
>
> (Luke 22:19–20)

Someone has called the Lord's Supper a "progressive dinner party." Each time we participate in the service, we are reminded that it is just another session of the same meal that began in the Upper Room when Jesus first broke bread with His disciples in this way. It has continued throughout time since then, reminding us of His death on our behalf.

This practice was assigned to the church so that we would regularly and perpetually remind ourselves of the blood that Jesus shed at Calvary. The breaking of the bread and the drinking of the cup constantly refreshes in us the memory and personal importance of His body and blood.

But this fellowship meal also looks forward. It commemorates Jesus's death *"till He comes"* (1 Corinthians 11:26). In a marvelous way, it anticipates the wedding feast of the Lamb of God in eternity. It spiritually unites us with all the saints of the past, present, and future.

The bread that we partake of in this sacrament represents the incarnation of the Bread of Life. The incarnation was God Himself, in Jesus, taking on a fleshly body, living among men, and offering His body in sacrifice for them. The cup, or the wine, represents the shedding of Jesus's blood as the means of God's establishing a new covenant with His people.

Through God's revelations to me concerning the blood, I have come to understand that it is the consistent and perpetual sharing of the bread and the cup that keeps our hearts and minds refreshed in the salvation provided for us by Jesus at Calvary. No other body or blood could make such a sacrifice. No other man or woman could claim such perfection as a spotless lamb before God. In every instance in which we partake of the bread and cup, we are saying to God, "I deserved to die, but I acknowledge the fact that Jesus took my place!"

Lest the sacrifice that Jesus made somehow be forgotten, and we begin to rest in the benefits of salvation without remembering its terrible price, we are to remind ourselves of the body of Jesus that was torn, battered, and pierced for us. We are to remember each tear in His flesh, each stripe in His back, and each time He was pierced as He provided our peace with God. The bread recounts for us these sufferings He bore in His body—sufferings that were rightfully ours, but which He willingly bore in our stead.

The same holds true for the cup. When we drink of the cup, we are to remind ourselves of the blood Jesus shed in Herod's palace, in Pilate's hall, and on Calvary's brow.

Oh, my friend, every time you drink the cup in the Lord's Supper, you should remind yourself of His blood. It was His blood instead of yours. His blood paid the price that made it possible for you to be forgiven. Forgiveness requires us to remember His blood and accept it as the only atoning sacrifice for our sins.

PEACE WITH OTHERS

The Lord's Supper is also a reminder of the peace and communion we have with others through Christ.

The cup of blessing which we bless, is it not the communion of the blood of Christ? The bread which we break, is it not the communion of the body of Christ? For we, though many, are one bread and one body; for we all partake of that one bread. Observe Israel after the flesh: Are not those who eat of the sacrifices partakers of the altar? (1 Corinthians 10:16–18)

The foundation of our peace with others is our having made peace with God through the blood of the cross. This reconciliation with God puts us in relationship with Him and enables us to live in peace, which is a fruit of His Spirit. Since God is our Father, all believers belong to the same family. Moreover, since all human beings are made in the image of God, we are to treat them with respect. *"And this commandment we have from Him: that he who loves God must love his brother also"* (1 John 4:21).

Underlying Cain's murder of his brother, Abel, was that he did not want to acknowledge his responsibility for loving and caring for his brother. *"Am I my brother's keeper?"* (Genesis 4:9) Cain asked defensively after he went out and killed him. In contrast, Christ came to earth as our Elder Brother and laid down His life for us to demonstrate how we are to love and treat others. John wrote,

> *But if we walk in the light as He is in the light, we have fellowship with one another, and the blood of Jesus Christ His Son cleanses us from all sin.*
>
> (1 John 1:7)

When we walk in the light, or truth, of our salvation, we can have fellowship with those around us. As we do this, the blood of Jesus will cleanse us from all sin.

THE FOUNDATION OF OUR
PEACE WITH OTHERS IS OUR
HAVING MADE PEACE WITH GOD
THROUGH THE BLOOD OF THE
CROSS. THIS RECONCILIATION
WITH GOD PUTS US IN
RELATIONSHIP WITH HIM AND
ENABLES US TO LIVE IN PEACE,
WHICH IS A FRUIT OF HIS SPIRIT.

Not only does the power of the blood apply to the personal realm of peacemaking, but it also extends to peace between people groups and nations. The blood of Jesus has the power to unite people of every race, culture, and ethnicity. It makes them a new people—the covenant people of God.

One of the truly remarkable scenes in heaven will be the throng, made up of people from all over the world, that will assemble before the throne of God:

> *After these things I looked, and behold, a great multitude which no one could number, of all nations, tribes, peoples, and tongues, standing before the throne and before the Lamb, clothed with white robes, with palm branches in their hands, and crying out with a loud voice, saying, "Salvation belongs to our God who sits on the throne, and to the Lamb!"*
>
> (Revelation 7:9–10)

Those who—on a natural plane—lived an existence characterized by deadly enmity before they made peace with their enemies through Christ demonstrate the truth that "[God] *has made from one blood every nation of men to dwell on all the face of the earth*" (Acts 17:26). This is not only a physical reality, but also a spiritual one that the evil of the world has impeded through the centuries. However, this reality of peaceful unity is fulfilled anew by the power of the blood of the Lamb.

Conflict between races and nationalities has existed since the beginning of history. It is easy to divide and bring enmity between people, but only the blood of the precious Lamb of God has the power to make peace and bring them together permanently. Paul was writing about the age-old conflict between Jews and Gentiles when he said,

> [Jesus] *Himself is our peace, who has made both one, and has broken down the middle wall of separation, having abolished in His flesh the enmity, that is, the law of commandments contained in ordinances, so as to create in Himself one new man from the two, thus making peace, and that He might reconcile them both to God in one body through the cross, thereby putting to death the enmity.* (Ephesians 2:14–16)

The gospel has had from its outset the stated goal of unifying people of all races and nationalities before God, and it is the blood of Christ that brings us together. There are countless brothers and sisters all over the world who come together and regularly celebrate in communion the memory of the blood of Christ, and we are united with them.

Men have forever tried through force of arms to unite different peoples into empires, but they have always ultimately failed. Yet the kingdom of Christ has lasted two thousand years because of the power of His blood.

His blood has transformed whole peoples. Visitors today can go to lands once dominated by cannibalism and heathen practices and find people living harmoniously because of the influence of the gospel. History records the account of a ship-wrecked people who survived unknown for decades on a lonely island in the Pacific Ocean. When discovered, it was revealed that they had decided to be governed by the principles of the New Testament they had carried ashore from the wreck of their ship. The result was a peaceable, happy, well-adjusted, wonderfully functioning community. Heaven will tell the stories of countless tribes and nations transformed by the power of the blood.

THE PEACE OF FORGIVENESS

Another vital aspect of our peace through the blood of Christ is the presence of forgiveness in our lives—God's forgiveness of us, and the forgiveness we give and receive from other human beings.

Christ shed His blood so that God could forgive us for every sin we ever committed, and through His blood, He is able to forgive us if we sin now. He has not only provided for our forgiveness at salvation, but also for our ongoing forgiveness: *"If we walk in the light as He is in the light,…the blood of Jesus Christ His Son cleanses us from all sin"* (1 John 1:7). There is no sin, no wrong, no crime that the blood of Jesus cannot remove. This truth can comfort us whenever we agonize over our own sins and seek God's cleansing anew.

The blood of Jesus also provides us with the power to forgive others as we become conformed to the image of Christ. When Jesus was hanging on the cross, He prayed for those who had crucified Him: *"Father, forgive them, for they do not know what they do"* (Luke 23:34). The power of forgiveness and right relationships is in the blood of the Lamb. The Scripture says, *"If it is possible, as much as depends on you, live peaceably with all men"* (Romans 12:18).

THE GOSPEL OF PEACE—A GOSPEL OF RECONCILIATION

Finally, the blood of Christ gives us the ministry of reconciliation. As we have been forgiven and restored to God, we are to seek to bring others to Him for atonement and restoration, also. *"Now all things are of God, who has reconciled us to Himself through Jesus Christ, and has given us the ministry of reconciliation"* (2 Corinthians 5:18).

9

TRANSFORMATION THROUGH THE BLOOD

*"But we all, with unveiled face, beholding as in a
mirror the glory of the Lord, are being transformed
into the same image from glory to glory, just as by
the Spirit of the Lord."*
—2 Corinthians 3:18

A third aspect of the application of the blood of Jesus in
our lives is that it provides for our spiritual transformation
into the image of Christ. As the Bible puts it, *"For by one*

offering He **has perfected forever** *those who are* **being sanctified**" (Hebrews 10:14, emphasis added). Although we have been redeemed, we are also *"being transformed…from glory to glory"* (2 Corinthians 3:18).

We are not to simply rest upon the benefits of our first encounter with Christ's blood but are to reflect the changed life that is the promise of our salvation. Being born again is just the beginning.

OVERCOMING POWER

The blood of Jesus was shed for the remission of all your sins. It is also the agent that gives you the ability and power to overcome challenges and temptations. When things start going wrong in our lives, many of us either have a pity party or start condemning and accusing ourselves, saying such things as "Why does everything always happen to me?" or "Why do I always mess up?" Sometimes, we feel this way because the accuser of the brethren is harassing us. (See Revelation 12:10.) He whispers in our thoughts, "If you were *really* a Christian, you wouldn't have done that."

When this happens to you, you can rejoice because you have already been promised overcoming power. The accuser can be defeated because the blood of Jesus will cause you to triumph. Satan will come to tell you that you have failed and are no good. However, you can appropriate what God has given you to remove anything within you that is not godly and replace it with the nature of Christ.

> *Much more then, having now been justified by His blood, we shall be saved from wrath through Him. For if when we were enemies we were reconciled to God through the death of His Son, **much more, having been reconciled, we shall be saved by His life.** And not only that, but we also rejoice in God through our Lord Jesus Christ, through whom we have now received the reconciliation.*
>
> (Romans 5:9–11, emphasis added)

DAILY CLEANSING

One thing God has given us is the ability to receive daily cleansing of our sins, as well as attitudes that are contrary to His thoughts and ways. With the temptations of this world, we are susceptible to wandering, even sliding away from, the commitment we have made to Christ. That is why we need a daily cleansing in His blood. What a wonderful thought that the blood of Jesus cleanses us, even now, from all sin!

> *For if the blood of bulls and goats and the ashes of a heifer, sprinkling the unclean, sanctifies for the purifying of the flesh, how much more shall the blood of Christ, who through the eternal Spirit offered Himself*

ONE THING GOD HAS GIVEN
US IS THE ABILITY TO RECEIVE
DAILY CLEANSING OF OUR
SINS, AS WELL AS ATTITUDES
THAT ARE CONTRARY TO HIS
THOUGHTS AND WAYS. WITH
THE TEMPTATIONS OF THIS
WORLD, WE ARE SUSCEPTIBLE
TO WANDERING, EVEN SLIDING
AWAY FROM, THE COMMITMENT
WE HAVE MADE TO CHRIST.
THAT IS WHY WE NEED A DAILY
CLEANSING IN HIS BLOOD. WHAT
A WONDERFUL THOUGHT THAT
THE BLOOD OF JESUS CLEANSES
US, EVEN NOW, FROM ALL SIN!

without spot to God, **cleanse your conscience from**
dead works to serve the living God?
(Hebrews 9:13–14, emphasis added)

The great comfort to the believer in his daily walk is the present and continuous cleansing of the blood. Each day, ask Jesus to cleanse you afresh through His blood so that you can serve the living God.

DAILY PRAYER, CONFESSION, AND WORSHIP

Second, while the sacrificial system is no longer needed, we can still learn spiritual truths from its practices. As we come before the Lord in confession, forgiveness, worship, and intercession, we should remember the spirit behind some of the regulations that the Israelites followed. Here are a few examples:

1. Recall that the Hebrews sacrificed a burnt offering every morning and evening. These offerings were not just for propitiation (forgiveness), but also for wholehearted consecration to God, which we will talk more about shortly. As you pray, regularly rededicate yourself to your heavenly Father and His purposes, and rejoice in His presence.

2. Remember that the guilt offering was for the purpose of reconciliation between man and God and

man and man. Jesus spoke to this idea when He taught, "*If you bring your gift to the altar, and there remember that your brother has something against you, leave your gift there before the altar, and go your way. First be reconciled to your brother, and then come and offer your gift*" (Matthew 5:23–24). As you pray, if you remember that you are not in right relationship with someone, seek God's forgiveness and then seek to mend the relationship. If applicable, offer restitution.

3. The sin offering was given by those who had committed sin without realizing at the time that what they had done was wrong. David may have been thinking of this concept when he prayed, "*Search me, O God, and know my heart; try me, and know my anxieties; and see if there is any wicked way in me, and lead me in the way everlasting*" (Psalm 139:23–24). We can pray the same prayer and know that the blood of Christ eternally cleanses from all sin. "[Jesus] *bore our sins in His own body on the tree, that we, having died to sins, might live for righteousness*" (1 Peter 2:24).

TRIUMPHING OVER SIN AND TEMPTATION

Jesus's atoning death has removed sin's defilement and annulled sin's power. By bearing the punishment of sin even unto death, Jesus conquered the power of sin, robbed the enemy of his spoils, and made it possible for believers to experience the power of a godly life. Faith in His blood gives us divine life so that we can triumph over sin in our daily living. His blood removes our sin from God's sight and, again, cleanses our consciences from "*dead works*" (Hebrews 9:14).

CONSECRATING OUR LIVES TO GOD

God has purposes for us in this world, and He desires to remove everything that would prevent our commitment to them. In Leviticus 8, Aaron and his sons were consecrated to their work as priests. After the ram of consecration was sacrificed, Moses sprinkled its blood on the altar and put some of the blood on the tips of the priests' right ears and on their right thumbs and toes. This rite signified the consecration of their whole lives to God's service. Let's adapt this symbolism for the consecration of our own lives to Him:

+ The ear represents what we hear. All that we listen to— radio, television, CDs, DVDs, conversations—everything that enters our minds must be filtered through the precious blood of the Lamb.

+ The thumb represents every work and skill we are capable of doing. It represents our acts. Everything we do should be done for God's glory and in the strength of Christ.

+ The toe represents where we go. It stands for our purposes and plans as well as our daily walk with the Lord. Everywhere we go, we need to reflect the nature and purposes of God, which we have received through the blood of the Lamb.

Let's talk about another powerful member of the body—the tongue. When we ask for the covering of Christ's blood on our tongues, our speech, and our words, we are asking God to guard us against using our words for evil, lies, anger, gossip, and those idle words we are prone to speak. Jesus said,

> But I say to you that for every idle word men may speak, they will give account of it in the day of judgment. For by your words you will be justified, and by your words you will be condemned.
>
> (Matthew 12:36–37)

James, the brother of Jesus, wrote the following:

> See how great a forest a little fire kindles! And the tongue is a fire, a world of iniquity. The tongue is so set among our members that it defiles the whole body, and sets on fire the course of nature; and it is set on fire by hell....But no man can tame the tongue. It is an unruly evil, full of deadly poison.   (James 3:5–6, 8)

And the apostle Paul warned, "[Let us not] *complain, as some of* [the Israelites in the desert] *also complained, and were destroyed by the destroyer*" (1 Corinthians 10:10).

As we surrender to Christ's power within us by His blood, we have the ability to take an unruly tongue and make it an altar of praise and gratitude. *"Therefore by Him let us continually offer the sacrifice of praise to God, that is, the fruit of our lips, giving thanks to His name"* (Hebrews 13:15).

What we see, also, needs to be screened in light of the blood of Jesus Christ. This includes television, the Internet, magazines, videos, DVDs, movies, and books. Any pastime or pursuit that can turn our minds away from Christ's purposes and ways must be avoided. In Job 31:3, we read that Job made a covenant with his eyes so that he would do what was right in the sight of God. (See Job 31:1, 7–8.)

COMMITMENT TO TRANSFORMATION

When we commit to being transformed into the image of Christ, we are fulfilling much of the purpose of the redeeming blood of Jesus. We were purchased for God so that we may love and serve Him as Christ did. When the Israelites of Moses's day sacrificed the sin offering,

the burning of the fat of the sacrifice upon the altar as…a soothing aroma unto Jehovah (Lev. 4:31) was symbolic of the handing over of the better part of the man, the part that is susceptible of renewal, to the purifying fire of the divine holiness and love, in order that the inward man might be renewed from day to day by the Spirit of the Lord and at length be changed into the glory of the children of God.[1]

In a similar way, we can hand over our lives to God in order to experience the purifying and renewing of His holiness and love. In this way, our lives, also, will reflect the glory of God through the blood of the Lamb.

10

HEALING THROUGH
THE BLOOD

"By his wounds you have been healed."
—1 Peter 2:24 (NIV)

I thank God for the precious blood that was shed on the cross many years ago so that you and I could be redeemed from the curse of the law and live for God in His grace. This is not wishful thinking but a spiritual reality. It took the blood of Jesus Christ being shed on the cross for us to be able to receive peace, healing, and deliverance. The supernatural

WHENEVER YOU SPEAK THE AUTHORITY OF THE BLOOD OF JESUS CHRIST AND ACTUATE THE POWER OF THE COVENANT OF GOD, A BATTLE WILL GO ON IN THE HEAVENS AND ON THE EARTH. WHEN YOU STAND BOLDLY AND PROCLAIM THE WORD OF THE LIVING GOD, THEREFORE, KNOW THAT THINGS WILL HAPPEN: IN THE NAME OF JESUS, DEMONS WILL FLEE AND DISEASES WILL BE HEALED. THROUGH THE BLOOD, MANY MIRACLES, SIGNS, AND WONDERS WILL OCCUR THROUGH THE PRAYERS OF HIS PEOPLE.

influence of God comes against the supernatural influence of the enemy. The spiritual powers of God hit the forces of the devil head-on, and the devil's works crumble.

OUR GREAT HEALER

Whenever you speak the authority of the blood of Jesus Christ and actuate the power of the covenant of God, a battle will go on in the heavens and on the earth. When you stand boldly and proclaim the Word of the living God, therefore, know that things will happen: In the name of Jesus, demons will flee and diseases will be healed. Through the blood, many miracles, signs, and wonders will occur through the prayers of His people.

Earlier, we saw that blood is the protector of the physical body. It fights illness and disease. It is the body's frontline defense against germs, bacteria, and harmful microorganisms. It provides an organized resistance against anything that is harmful to the body.

Similarly, the precious blood of the Lamb protects those who are covered by the blood. He gives life and health because He is the Great Healer. Many times, I have seen the sick and lame healed through the name of Jesus and the blood of the cross.

HEALED BY HIS STRIPES

One day, the Spirit of God spoke to me and told me to go to the children's hospital to pray for someone. I didn't know anyone who was admitted to that hospital, but I obeyed the Lord. His Spirit led me down a hallway to where I heard a child crying. I entered the child's room and tried to comfort him. Jesus said to me, "Lay your hands on his stomach and plead My blood covenant over him."

I obeyed the Lord, and the child went to sleep. The doctors did more X-rays and found that the little boy was completely healed. The blood of Jesus Christ had done its work. Isaiah the prophet proclaimed,

> *He was wounded for our transgressions, He was bruised for our iniquities; the chastisement for our peace was upon Him, and by His stripes we are healed.* (Isaiah 53:5)

With every stripe that tore into the flesh of His back, He provided for multitudes of illnesses, diseases, and injuries to be healed. Blind eyes and deaf ears were opened with every stripe. Mute tongues were loosed, the lame walked, and all types of deformities were transformed with every swing of the scourger's whip.

On another occasion, I was casting out spirits, as well as binding and loosing, when I became grieved because the person I was praying for at that particular time didn't seem to be getting any better. The Spirit of the Lord began to impress on me that I should plead the precious blood of the Lamb.

I began to say, "By the life and power of the blood of Christ Jesus, I take dominion over you, Satan. In the name of the Lord, you're going to loose this person and let him go. By the blood of the Lamb that He shed to deliver us from the power of the enemy, I claim healing."

As I pleaded the blood and claimed healing, I began to see an immediate change in the person. Many times since then, I've used this prayer as the Holy Spirit inspires me to. By the power of the blood of Jesus, the demons loose people and let them go. The power of God heals and mends them. I've even seen tissues repaired.

Rebuke Satan through the blood of the Lamb, and he has to flee. The enemy cannot stay when you boldly proclaim the Word of God. By Jesus's stripes—those powerful stripes that He took for our healing—His power is as real today as it ever was. His blood will never lose its power!

11

DELIVERANCE THROUGH THE BLOOD

*"They overcame [Satan] by the blood of the Lamb
and by the word of their testimony."*
—Revelation 12:11

In the many revelations God has given me concerning the blood of the Lamb, an enlightening hope that has given me great strength and consolation is the fact that the blood is our defense for our lives and for spiritual warfare.

Through His blood, we are able to overcome the carnal nature that exists in each of us from birth. Through His blood, we are able to overcome the evil and enticing world around us; we can overcome the temptation to sin, false condemnation, and sin's power in our lives. And through His blood, we are able to overcome the enemy. We have the power and authority to walk upon the back of Satan and defeat him in every way.

Jesus's blood has freed the church, the new people of God, from the power of the devil and all evil power. Even when we pass through the valley of the shadow of death, His blood is sufficient to carry us through.

I was reading a book by Catherine of Siena, who also had a vision of the Lord and the day He was crucified. She saw Him arise in a glorified body from the sepulcher where He was laid. He was glorious and beautiful, and light glowed in the wounds of His hands.

She said the angels went with Him, and she saw demons bound in chains before Him. Catherine said that, in the vision, she saw the Lord standing full of power and strength. The devil appeared before Him like a dragon. They began to wrestle and fight in combat, and earthquakes shook the earth.

Then she saw the Lord take the dragon's head and put it under His heels and crush it. Finally, He pried the keys of death and hell out of the dragon's hand. She said all this was possible because of the blood He shed.[1]

THE TACTICS OF THE ENEMY

It's important that we first understand why we must battle the enemy. After God created a perfect world and sinless humanity, an ominous change took place. In Genesis 3, we read that the first man and woman, who were in communion with God, decided to establish a relationship with Satan, who was in rebellion against God.

Eve encountered Satan in the form of a serpent. She was deceived by the subtle temptations he offered her. Through the record of this biblical incident, God shows us that we can observe Satan's ultimate destructive intentions for mankind and the methods he employs in achieving that goal.

THE ENEMY'S NUMBER ONE GOAL: TO SEPARATE HUMANITY FROM GOD

Satan's number one goal is to separate human beings from God so that they will be ultimately destroyed. The reason for Satan's obvious hatred for mankind is found in Genesis 1:27: *"So God created man in His own image; in the image of God He created him; male and female He created them."*

Since the devil hates God so intensely, it is natural that this hatred would be extended to mankind, who is created in the image of God. Thus we became the object of Satan's attacks and torments. Since he cannot attack God directly,

Satan attacks Him by attacking His creation—especially the creature who was created with His nature.

This is why we should not be surprised when we become the target of the enemy's anger and hatred. A relationship was established between man and Satan that is somewhat like the relationship between a hungry lion and a vulnerable lamb. Since that fateful day when Adam and Eve listened to the serpent, Satan has been constantly stalking man *"like a roaring lion, seeking whom he may devour"* (1 Peter 5:8).

One night, I awoke and everything seemed to be covered in red—the walls, the floors, even what was outside. I looked out the window, and there was a hedge built around my home. The peace of God came, and His voice said, "I will be a wall of fire about you, daughter, and I will overshadow you, protect you, and watch over you. I will do this for all My children who love Me and keep My commandments."

I went back to sleep in the presence of God. I began to see fire, glory, and power, as the Word of God became alive. I could see what seemed to be the blood of Jesus covering things I didn't even know He was covering. It was like a protective shield. Wherever I go to preach and pray, I talk about the blood of the Lamb because it is the keeping power of God.

Because of the divine image of God in man, and because of the protective covering that Jesus provides believers through the blood, Satan's methods of attacking us are limited to enticement, temptation, and subterfuge. Yet these methods have been sufficient to entrap and enslave untold millions of human beings over the millennia. This is the tragedy of the ages!

SATAN'S SIMPLE TASK

In many ways, Satan's job is not difficult because every one of us gravitates toward sin. Satan cannot force sin upon us, but he can work subtly to get us to yield to it. Remember, however, that all he is empowered to do is to tempt, entice, and deceive. When we yield, it is the lust that rules our hearts that makes us disobey God. The Bible tells us,

> But each one is tempted when he is drawn away by his own desires and enticed. Then, when desire has conceived, it gives birth to sin; and sin, when it is full-grown, brings forth death.   (James 1:14–15)

Satan has made plans to ensnare you and me. Sometimes he will come subtly and sometimes he will assault openly. He operates throughout the realm we call the world. The world is the place where we live, think, and act. Our lives are played out like dramas twenty-four hours a day, seven days a week. We face overwhelming and seemingly insurmountable forces every day.

ATTACKED BY "PHILISTINES"

The ancient enemies of Israel, the Philistines, always attacked the people of God whenever they detected a weakness in them. The Scriptures depict the Philistines as representative of all the things of the world that obstruct, oppose, and enslave the people of God.

Likewise, Satan empowers and emboldens anyone who has the slightest tendency to want to attack God's people. He never gets discouraged, and he never loses his willingness to accuse, frustrate, and attempt to defeat the believer.

Yet there is good news! Jesus has given us the assurance in His Word that we are not powerless against the enemy's forces if we will put our faith in Him. No power exists that can touch anyone who rests in His will by faith. The prophet Isaiah said,

> *"No weapon formed against you shall prosper, and every tongue which rises against you in judgment you shall condemn. This is the heritage of the servants of the* LORD, *and their righteousness is from Me," says the* LORD.   (Isaiah 54:17)

I have learned that I have to come against the enemy in the name of the Lord of Hosts if I want to be victorious.

For though we walk in the flesh, we do not war accord-
ing to the flesh. For the weapons of our warfare are
not carnal but mighty in God for pulling down strong-
holds, casting down arguments and every high thing
that exalts itself against the knowledge of God, bring-
ing every thought into captivity to the obedience of
Christ.   (2 Corinthians 10:3–5)

The forces of evil and darkness are constantly challenging
the people of God. The boundary of the blood is the place of
continual conflict. There is no letup in the battle with evil.
Often, the enemy's spiritual opposition comes in the form of
human opposition. We have ongoing warfare with the enemies of morality in our society. We battle for truth. We fight
against wickedness and evil. We war against oppression and
injustice.

This never-ending confrontation with the enemy of our
souls is not only individual, but is also a battle for our families and nations. The illegal drug and pornography industries
are regiments in today's Philistine army. So are the abortion
mills. Those who promote violence and pervert morals are the
Philistines who stand at the boundary of the blood, plotting
to destroy our families and our country.

I believe it is time for believers to stand up and speak out.
It is not time for us to hold our peace in silence. Speak out
against evil. We need to stand publicly against the things that

tear down community standards and erode the moral fiber of our people. Whether we realize it or not, the enemy awaits us at the boundary of the blood every day.

One time, I was preaching in a service, and the Lord directed me to notice that there were many men present, and He gave me such compassion for them. I was preaching about perversion and the sins of our eyes, hands, and bodies. The Holy Spirit was dealing in a strong but kind way with the people. I was telling them that through the name of Jesus, there is hope. They could be delivered from any oppression or any evil spirit that was perplexing or tormenting them.

As I began to talk about the power of the name of Jesus and the blood of the Lamb, I saw a vision in the back of the church. It was a huge dove, and he was red and full of fire. As he flew about and flapped his wings, spectacular fireballs would come from him. As these fireballs dropped on the people, I saw that they were mixed with blood and vapors of smoke. Certain people would raise their hands and scream, "I want Jesus to set me free. I repent of my sins."

As people came to the altar, they would be purged and cleansed by the blood of the Lamb and the Word of God. It was a phenomenal and beautiful work of God. Hundreds were saved that day. As we proclaimed the Word of God, the power of the Holy Spirit came in and brought deliverance and hope.

We are living in a perverse generation. We must work with God in the power of His Holy Spirit, doing the will of the Father.

DELIVERANCE THROUGH THE CROSS

As I have preached at various churches, I have learned that, in every place where I saw a revelation of God's fire on the pulpit, deliverance would come. I would see angels touching the pulpit at various times and worshiping God. Often, I would see them holding one hand to heaven (sometimes both of them) as they magnified the Lord.

I kept returning to churches like this, and one day, during a service, the glory of God rolled in with a mighty revelation. I saw angels come into the church with a large cross that looked about fifteen feet high. They went to the pulpit, which appeared to be on fire. The angels seemed to dig around in the floor, and then they anchored the cross in front of the pulpit. The cross was solid, but fire shot out of both ends and the top of it. I saw this revelation several times, and each time, there would be a great deliverance. Many people would come to the altar, get saved, and be delivered in a marvelous way. It was an awesome sight.

I wondered about what I had seen, so I began to ask the Lord, "God, what is all of this? What does this mean in the holy Word of God?" He said to me,

These pulpits that you see with the fire upon them represent pulpits where My true Word is being preached. These holy, anointed ministers are purifying the flock with the Word of God and the cross that you see. Therefore, I have established the cross there, and the Spirit is with them for the purposes of deliverance and for the Word of God to be fulfilled. This is a sign that things will happen that they have been asking Me to do, and it means they are preaching the pure, holy Word of God through the eternal and mighty power of the cross.

All over the land, I would see the same revelation. Again, as I observed the angels in action, it was almost like watching a movie screen. In many places, I would see angels come in like a cleanup crew and begin to sweep evil powers out of the churches. They would break the bonds of people and liberate them.

At one service, some people took pictures, and when they were developed, you could see fire around the people we were praying for. It was a brilliant red in color, and I was excited because it showed the revelation knowledge of the blood of Jesus Christ. It was awesome for me to see these angels working in the spirit realm for God. While it excited me to see these things happen, they did not occur in all the churches or all the meetings.

One day, I was in prayer when the Lord began to talk to me about the revelations He was giving to me.

My child, you must learn that many times I will open up a vision to you, and what I'm showing you is not present right there before you. It will be for the future, or it will be happening in another part of the world. You were given the vision so that you can intercede. Listen to Me, and I will give you instructions on how to pray.

Sometimes, people will receive a revelation, and they will think that what is happening is right there beside their beds. They will think that what they are seeing is there in the room with them, but it is not so. I am a holy God, and I am protective of My children. I am revealing truth and mysteries to you so you can reveal them to the world.

I'm showing you one of the workings of the enemy, Satan, so that you can pray; and the blood that I shed—the blood covenant—will come and stop the flow of these channels, these avenues, of the devil.

I was so excited! I said, "Okay, Lord."

Time went by, and one day, I was in Phoenix to preach the gospel. Some of us had been in intercessory prayer for the city.

We had prayed and gone to sleep, but I awoke at three o'clock in the morning. I felt as though I had been awake for hours.

I looked at the ceiling, and I could see something appearing before my eyes. A manifestation of a spiritual object came through the ceiling and hovered around in a circle. At one end of the object, I could see a small opening that measured about eight inches by twelve inches. I saw that the tiny opening was a door.

As I looked through this door, I could see a witch with a crystal ball sitting at a table. I knew that she could see from the crystal ball into the place where I was. I also knew that God had allowed me to see what I was seeing, and that He had allowed her to be able to do this in order to show me how to pray. I took in this whole scenario very quickly. Then the door shut, and the thing moved right out of the room.

I got up and said, "Lord, what in the world was that?" God said to me,

I'm showing you strategy of the devil. Many witches and warlocks work for the devil in this area, and they have these crystal balls. They have figured out how to go through the airways and spy out the land in certain areas where My blood does not provide a covering. A blood covering can be provided only through prayer and through believing in Me and the covenant of God. Many do not believe in My protection as you do.

When My righteousness covers My children and they are living holy lives before Me, when they are doing the best they can, My covenant—the atonement—stands for them and their families. No matter where they are, no matter where their children are, a hedge of protection surrounds them.

Many do not believe this, but I know you do. I've proven this to you many times over with your own children and your family. Many times, I've saved your family from harmful things that crossed their paths.

My covenant—the atonement for the healing of the body, the blood that I shed over two thousand years ago—still stands today. My covenant promises are for you and your children.

The armlike object you saw, with the opening and a small door at the front of it, was a passageway from the crystal ball through the spirit realm to where you are in this home.

I allowed you to see this hovering in the atmosphere in order to teach you to pray. Watch closely, and I'll show you something else.

God then showed me what looked like a huge television screen. I could see a woman's face, and I would recognize her now if I could see her in the flesh. She was clearly visible, and she was hovering over a crystal ball and screaming in a loud voice. Then the devil came roaring and screaming into the place where she was. "Why did you let her see you?" Satan yelled. "Why did you let her see you?"

The woman and the devil began arguing. This led to fighting and more yelling. I heard the devil tell this wicked woman that she had a big mouth and would tell everybody. The devil—his form was huge—grabbed the wall and started roaring and screaming in anger. Then he went through the door, and the Lord suddenly spoke to me,

Plead My blood! Plead the blood of Jesus! Plead the blood that I shed. The life and the power of the blood of Jesus that was shed two thousand years ago has never lost its power over situations like these. The blood has power over those crystal balls that are the spirit realm's venues of sin; it can shut those doors.

I did just as the Lord said because I believed Him. When I began to pray, I saw fire mixed with blood. I saw vapors of smoke. I saw the power of God shoot through the atmosphere and explode the woman's crystal ball. She screamed and ran all over the room; as the power of God hit again, she ran out of the room.

The Lord told me, "Pray in every area where I send you as you have just done here. Pray right now for others who have these crystal balls."

So I prayed for a long time. He showed me how to pray. His angels taught me how to pray through the Scriptures, how to bind and loose (see Matthew 18:18), how to plead His precious blood, and how to rely on the Word of God. Every time I would do these things, there would be a great deliverance among the people. In the spiritual realm, I saw the angels scatter many of the enemies of God's people. In one vision, I saw what looked like ten thousand scattered at one time.

I also saw people delivered who were in supernatural bondage. It was as though ropes and vines had grown around them, but when the fire hit them, the shackles would explode. I knew that God was showing me these mighty revelations through the power of His Holy Spirit. I thought, *God, You are such a wonderful God.*

Then I saw the dove of the Holy Spirit soaring through the heavens. God began to draw people by His Spirit, and I was so happy and excited to see the blessings and joy of the Lord. I truly began to understand that we are in a spiritual war where good is fighting against evil.

RECLAIMING WHAT SATAN HAS STOLEN

I have also found that the enemy often encroaches on our praise territory. He intrudes into our private worship, mocking the things of God. He invades the realm of praise. If we allow it, he will occupy places where he does not belong. He brashly invades God's territory and plans to take everything we allow him to take. We don't have to surrender to the enemy, however. The blood of Jesus makes it possible for us to reclaim what Satan, through deceit and trickery, has taken from us. In Christ, we can experience peace in this world.

> *For it pleased the Father that in Him all the fullness should dwell, and by Him to reconcile all things to Himself, by Him, whether things on earth or things in heaven, having made peace through the blood of His cross.* (Colossians 1:19–20)

Once I was praying for a girl who was only twelve years old. She had been attacked and molested. As I was praying for her, I felt led to have someone take a picture. I had her stand against the wall for the photograph. When the pictures were developed, the whole wall was covered in red. The Lord said, "That was my blood washing the child clean." Praise God for the blood of the Lamb!

I believe that my calling in God is to confront the lies of the devil. In many countries and islands of the world, I have done just that. I remember a time when my own child was using drugs, and I was praying for the power of Jesus to set him free. I actually saw the battle in the heavens as the devil and the demons fought the angels of God over my son.

I began to pray, and the Holy Spirit gave me the ability and the words to say, "The power and the life and the blood of Jesus Christ, which was shed on Calvary two thousand years ago, has never lost its power," and I would claim the Word of God for him. I would stand on the Word and stand against the devil as the Word would go forth. I saw the Word make the devil and the evil spirits back down. God would intervene for my son every time through the blood of the Lamb.

On one particular day, my spirit was raging because of spiritual warfare. I was earnestly interceding to God for a spiritual battle. At times, I would literally groan in my spirit as I poured out my soul to God. Weeping tears of contrition, I pleaded with God for His deliverance. I had contacted some other people I had confidence in, some genuine prayer warriors, to intercede with me.

Suddenly, God spoke to me. Whether it was an audible voice that I heard or a strong impression in my spirit, I do not know. All I know is that it was a distinct voice, clear and unmistakable. This is what He spoke to me:

Take heart, My child; stand firm in the boundary of blood. You need not struggle; for I, the Lord your God, will fight your battle for you.

In an instant, my burdens were lifted. It seemed as if the sun had suddenly broken through a very dark and foreboding cloud. I could pray with liberty and freedom. My spirit was soaring, and my heart was overflowing with joy. I remembered the verse that says,

Therefore, brethren, having boldness to enter the Holiest by the blood of Jesus, by a new and living way which He consecrated for us, through the veil, that is, His flesh, and having a High Priest over the house of God, let us draw near with a true heart in full assurance of faith, having our hearts sprinkled from an evil conscience and our bodies washed with pure water.

(Hebrews 10:19–22)

THE VALLEY OF BLOOD

A story in the Old Testament tells of a time when the kings of Judah, Israel, and Edom were aligned against their enemy, the Moabites. (See 2 Kings 3.) The situation looked hopeless, and it seemed as if they were facing certain disaster. The kings sought advice from the prophet of God, and Elisha told them to dig the valley full of ditches. God would fill the ditches with water, although it would not rain and the wind would not blow. Further, He would give them victory over the Moabites.

Although they didn't understand the strange request, they obeyed God and dug the valley full of ditches. When the Moabite army heard that Judah, Israel, and Edom were coming, they marched confidently out to confront them. Early in the morning, they stormed through a mountain pass and suddenly saw what looked like a valley filled with blood. The ditches were full of water, and the rising sun glimmering on the waters caused the scene to appear to be a vast valley of blood.

The Moabites concluded, incorrectly, that the armies of Judah, Israel, and Edom had defeated each other so they ran forward to take the spoils. The people of God, however, waited in ambush and won a glorious victory.

The valley of blood is a symbol of victory for the believer. Christ's blood always routs the enemy; the devil flees from it. I have often pleaded the blood against an enemy or a negative situation and seen firsthand the power of God at work. The blood of Christ has never lost its power. Its strength is available for every believer.

The following are several verses from the Bible that talk about our ability to have victory over the enemy and our sinful nature:

THE VALLEY OF BLOOD IS A
SYMBOL OF VICTORY FOR THE
BELIEVER. CHRIST'S BLOOD
ALWAYS ROUTS THE ENEMY;
THE DEVIL FLEES FROM IT. I
HAVE OFTEN PLEADED THE
BLOOD AGAINST AN ENEMY OR A
NEGATIVE SITUATION AND SEEN
FIRSTHAND THE POWER OF GOD
AT WORK. THE BLOOD OF CHRIST
HAS NEVER LOST ITS POWER.
ITS STRENGTH IS AVAILABLE FOR
EVERY BELIEVER.

Submit to God. Resist the devil and he will flee from
you.   (James 4:7)

"Be angry, and do not sin": do not let the sun go down
on your wrath, nor give place to the devil.
                                            (Ephesians 4:26–27)

Therefore do not let sin reign in your mortal body,
that you should obey it in its lusts. And do not pres-
ent your members as instruments of unrighteousness
to sin, but present yourselves to God as being alive
from the dead, and your members as instruments of
righteousness to God. For sin shall not have dominion
over you, for you are not under law but under grace.
                                            (Romans 6:12–14)

Do you not know that friendship with the world is
enmity with God? Whoever therefore wants to be a
friend of the world makes himself an enemy of God.
                                                    (James 4:4)

The enemy will take what we will give him through our
indifference, neglect, disobedience, and compromise. It is up
to us to stand firm and resist the temptations of the devil. Jesus
Christ, the precious Lamb of God, stands at the boundary of

blood as our great Conqueror. He is there to fight our battles for us and to help us slay all the giants in our paths.

OVERCOMING BLOOD

When Jesus died on Calvary, He opened up for us the fountain of His life's blood. With that blood, we overcome the powers of darkness—the devil and the entire spiritual underworld. The blood is God's trophy that celebrates Christ's victory over death, hell, and the grave. Jesus said, *"I am He who lives, and was dead, and behold, I am alive forevermore. Amen. And I have the keys of Hades and of Death"* (Revelation 1:18). His blood may not be visible to you and me, but you can be sure that demons and all other unclean spirits can see it. They are terrified by the blood. They run from it. They cannot remain in the presence of the blood of Jesus Christ.

Satan had no idea that the death of Christ would bring about his defeat, although prophets had predicted it for centuries. Paul called this truth *"a mystery"* or *"hidden wisdom."*

> *But we speak the wisdom of God in a mystery, the hidden wisdom which God ordained before the ages for our glory, which none of the rulers of this age knew; for had they known, they would not have crucified the Lord of glory.* (1 Corinthians 2:7–8)

Satan and his demons failed utterly at Calvary; they lost their claim on our souls. The blood of Jesus is an eternal reminder to them of their failed mission. The immoral, spiritual underworld has diminished and hollow abilities now. Its strength was made null and void on the day Jesus died. They are now powerless over the souls of believers because of the blood of Jesus Christ.

This is why believers "plead the blood" when they are in a heated spiritual battle with the enemy. Paul explained the victory of the believer through Christ's blood:

> And you, being dead in your trespasses and the uncircumcision of your flesh, He has made alive together with Him, having forgiven you all trespasses, having wiped out the handwriting of requirements that was against us, which was contrary to us. And He has taken it out of the way, having nailed it to the cross. Having disarmed principalities and powers, He made a public spectacle of them, triumphing over them in it. (Colossians 2:13–15)

In another vision about the blood of the Lamb, I was praying about a particular matter, and we were being attacked by evil powers. We were praying for people in the church, and there were many attacks of the devil—strange things happening, puzzling things for which we had no answer. The Spirit of the Lord fell on me, and we started singing:

By the life and the power and the blood of
Christ Jesus,
Satan, you have to go!
In the name of Jesus, He will make you whole.
Through the blood of the Lamb that was shed
on Calvary
So many years ago,
It's never lost its power.
By the life and the power of Christ Jesus,
you've got to go!

As we sang, there was a spiritual lifting and a freedom in the room where we were praying. It was through the blood of the Lamb that we got victory that day.

The blood of Christ is so powerful that it also protects us from the "angel of death":

Now the blood shall be a sign for you on the houses where you are. And when I see the blood, I will pass over you; and the plague shall not be on you to destroy you when I strike the land of Egypt. (Exodus 12:13)

This passage is referring to real, physical death. The angel of death passed through the land, executing God's judgment against the Egyptians, slaying the firstborn. Thousands died that night in homes that did not have the blood applied to their doorposts. But the people who believed obeyed the

Lord's command, applied the blood, and were spared God's wrath.

In a similar way, when the blood is applied spiritually to our souls, we are safe from the Second Death, which is eternal separation from God. Jesus said, *"Whoever lives and believes in Me shall never die"* (John 11:26). Yet He also said,

> But the cowardly, unbelieving, abominable, murderers, sexually immoral, sorcerers, idolaters, and all liars shall have their part in the lake which burns with fire and brimstone, which is the second death.
>
> (Revelation 21:8)

Thank God, we can overcome the temptation to sin, we can overcome the past, and we can overcome Satan—all enemies that try to destroy us—*"by the blood of the Lamb and by the word of [our] testimony"* (Revelation 12:11). Don't let the enemy rob you of the truth of what defeats him.

Sin is still costly. Man's inhumanity to man costs us more in human lives than we are willing to admit. But the sacrifices in the violent streets of our cities and on the war-ravaged battlefields of the world will never break the hold sin has on humanity.

Only Christ's blood can do this. Oh, the wonderful power of His blood! It has utterly destroyed the power of sin, death, the grave, and hell. The power of Jesus's blood has opened

WHEN SATAN, THE BRASH BULLY
OF THE WORLD, STEPS OUT TO
CHALLENGE GOD'S CAUSE, YOU
CAN KNOW THAT THE BLOOD
OF CHRIST PROVIDES EVERY
BELIEVER WITH THE NECESSARY
PROVISION TO DEFEAT HIM. I
CANNOT EXPRESS THE JOY THAT
FILLS ME WHEN I THINK ABOUT
THE OVERCOMING POWER THAT
IS MADE POSSIBLE BY THE BLOOD
OF THE LAMB!

heaven for all to come who will. *"Having now been justified by His blood, we shall be saved from wrath through Him"* (Romans 5:9).

The theme of this chapter and the thrust of what God has revealed to me is that Jesus, our wonderful Lord and Savior, meets Satan, the flesh, and the world at the boundary of blood. Just as the Israelites did not have to fight if they trusted that God would fight for them—if they knew that *"the battle is the* LORD'*s"* (1 Samuel 17:47)—so Jesus today fights our battles for us. He has shed His blood so that sin no longer has dominion over the believer who trusts completely in Him.

When Satan, the brash bully of the world, steps out to challenge God's cause, you can know that the blood of Christ provides every believer with the necessary provision to defeat him. I cannot express the joy that fills me when I think about the overcoming power that is made possible by the blood of the Lamb!

Then I heard a loud voice saying in heaven, "Now salvation, and strength, and the kingdom of our God, and the power of His Christ have come, for the accuser of our brethren, who accused them before our God day and night, has been cast down. And they overcame him by the blood of the Lamb and by the

> word of their testimony, and they did not love their
> lives to the death." (Revelation 12:10–11)

All our lives, we are bombarded by the attacks of an enemy who relentlessly comes against us with accusations. He does his diabolical work before we get saved, and it seems as if his attacks intensify when we recognize that Jesus is *"the Lamb of God who takes away the sin of the world"* (John 1:29).

John, in Revelation 12, properly named him *"the accuser"* (verse 10) and pictured him accusing God's people before Him day and night. We don't know all the forms that his accusations take, except that we have seen how he came against Job, and we know that Jesus revealed that he is a liar and the Father of Lies. (See John 8:44.) I know of times when godly people have been falsely accused on earth, and this has resulted in confusion and fears; therefore, I don't put anything past the chief slanderer.

The grand truth that gives us all cause for rejoicing is that the blood of the Lamb will eventually destroy and cast down the accuser. The blood, coupled with the believer's testimony, guarantees that he or she will become an overcomer.

Think of it! Because of the saving blood of Christ, the accuser is cast down. Satan's back is broken. The above Scripture from Revelation speaks of the time when, once and for all, the slanderer will be cowed and defeated.

This assurance should encourage every child of God to confidently plead the blood of the Lamb and boldly testify to His mighty power. Oh, there's power in the name of Jesus, and there's power in the blood of the Lamb!

12

THE BLOOD AND
THE KINGDOM

*"To Him who loved us...and has made us kings and
priests to His God and Father."*
—Revelation 1:5–6

T he record of the beginning of Jesus's ministry significantly includes the announcement that He came preaching the gospel of the kingdom:

Now after John was put in prison, Jesus came to Galilee, preaching the gospel of the kingdom of God, and saying, "The time is fulfilled, and the kingdom of God is at hand. Repent, and believe in the gospel."

(Mark 1:14–15)

The atoning blood of Jesus does not have as its purpose only our salvation, although that is its first and most momentous result. God also has in mind the building of His kingdom. In the heavenly Father's plan, there is a connection between our being redeemed by the blood of Christ and His kingdom, in which He has given us a significant role. We see this connection in the following Scriptures:

*Jesus Christ, the faithful witness, the firstborn from the dead, and the ruler over the kings of the earth. To Him who loved us and **washed us from our sins in His own blood,** and **has made us kings and priests to His God and Father**, to Him be glory and dominion forever and ever. Amen.*

(Revelation 1:5–6, emphasis added)

*You are worthy to take the scroll, and to open its seals; for You were slain, and have redeemed us to God by Your blood out of every tribe and tongue and people and nation, and have **made us kings and priests to***

our God; and we shall reign on the earth.

(Revelation 5:9–10, emphasis added)

Through the blood of Christ, we have become *"kings and priests"* to our heavenly Father. As kings, we are to promote justice and the ways of God in the earth. As priests, we are to carry out our ministry of reconciliation, bringing others to God through our Great High Priest, the Mediator of the new covenant.

GOD'S KINGDOM PEOPLE

God has always had a people. The people of Israel, the descendants of Abraham, had been set free from Egyptian slavery by a series of miracles under the leadership of Moses. In the thirteenth century before Christ, led by Moses's successor, Joshua, they had conquered Canaan and inhabited the land God had promised them.

The inauguration of this "kingdom people" was accomplished by blood. Exodus 24 tells the experience of Moses coming down from the mountain where he had received the law of God and calling together the people to bind them into a covenant relationship with God. It was an alliance sealed with blood:

Moses came and told the people all the words of the LORD and all the judgments. And all the people answered with one voice and said, "All the words which the LORD has said we will do."...Then he sent young men of the children of Israel, who offered burnt offerings and sacrificed peace offerings of oxen to the LORD....And Moses took the blood, sprinkled it on the people, and said, "This is the blood of the covenant which the LORD has made with you according to all these words." (Exodus 24:3, 5, 8)

Although the phrase *kingdom of God* is an expression unique to the New Testament, the concept of the people of God living under His kingship in a covenant relationship is an ancient one. The kingdom that God wished to establish with obedient people began when they offered sacrifices. The shedding of blood signified their willingness to enter into covenant with Him, and their being sprinkled by the blood set them apart as God's covenant people.

The "kingdom" in its infancy took its first political shape after the conquest of Canaan and further developed under the successive kingships of Saul, David, and Solomon. Israel and Judah, which existed as both united and separate entities, were earthly expressions of the spiritual idea of a called-out people living under the ultimate kingship of God Himself.

THE MESSAGE OF THE PROPHETS

The prophets of Israel understood—much better, apparently, than the people themselves—the spiritual nature of the kingdom of God. They realized that God intended for the citizens of the kingdom to live lives marked by righteousness and justice. A remarkable series of these men of God over a period of nearly a millennium repeatedly charged the imperfect followers of Jehovah to change their ways and live as God intended.

Although I could quote any number of the prophets testifying of the failures of God's people to live up to their calling, Jeremiah is representative of those who recognized how far the people fell short of God's expectations and who continually exhorted them to holy living.

The Weeping Prophet, as Jeremiah came to be known, condemned ungodly conduct and challenged Israel to live up to her calling. Perhaps clearer than some of the other prophets, he looked forward to a new day and a new covenant that would replace the failed relationship that existed between the people and their God. He had a realistic vision of the new kingdom brought into being by God's coming King.

"Behold, the days are coming," says the LORD, "That I will raise to David a Branch of righteousness; a King shall reign and prosper, and execute judgment and

righteousness in the earth. In His days Judah will be saved, and Israel will dwell safely; now this is His name by which He will be called: THE LORD OUR RIGHTEOUSNESS.*"* (Jeremiah 23:5–6)

Other notable prophets, such as Amos and Hosea, reiterated the same message: God desires to have a people who will live up to His desires and expectations for them.

The prophet Zechariah strikingly foretold the coming of the Messiah, who would set up an ultimate kingdom whose *"dominion shall be 'from sea to sea.'"* (See Zechariah 9:9–11.) Zechariah reminded his hearers that—although they had been unfaithful to it—they were still part of a covenant that had been established by blood. He wrote, *"As for you also, because of the blood of your covenant, I will set your prisoners free from the waterless pit"* (Zechariah 9:11).

Along with their thunderous warnings of judgment if the people failed to follow God, the prophets shared with their hearers the promises of the blessings of God if they would repent and turn back to Him. For the most part, their message seemed to fall on deaf ears. Occasionally, though, the Bible reports of a remnant who clung to the Word of God.

It is a faithful remnant in the New Testament who, hearing the message of the Messiah Himself and accepting it, would be the first to enter into the New Israel, the long-awaited kingdom of God.

THE CHARACTER OF THE KINGDOM

The kingdom of God is manifestly different from any earthly kingdom. Its distinctives lie in the manner in which people become citizens, the laws that govern their daily existence, and its ultimate outcome.

BORN OF BLOOD

The only way a person can become a citizen of the kingdom of God is to born into it, but not with a natural birth. Jesus taught, *"You must be born again"* (John 3:7). Speaking later to His followers, He was more specific about the role that identifying with His death would play in their salvation and entrance into the kingdom:

> Then Jesus said to them, *"Most assuredly, I say to you, unless you eat the flesh of the Son of Man and drink His blood, you have no life in you. Whoever eats My flesh and drinks My blood has eternal life, and I will raise him up at the last day. For My flesh is food indeed, and My blood is drink indeed. He who eats My flesh and drinks My blood abides in Me, and I in him."* (John 6:53–56)

This saying of Jesus puzzled those who heard it, and some among them attempted to understand it literally. From the perspective of the institution of the Lord's Supper, however, it

BY IDENTIFYING WITH THE
SACRIFICE OF HIS BODY
AND BLOOD ON THE CROSS,
BELIEVERS CAN EXPERIENCE A
NEW BIRTH, BORN OF BLOOD—
NOT A NATURAL BIRTH,
BUT A SPIRITUAL NEW
CREATION MADE POSSIBLE BY
HIS BLOOD SACRIFICE.

is easy to understand that He was speaking of a relationship of identification with His sacrifice.

Jesus was by no means advocating a kind of first-century cannibalism; He was simply saying that by identifying with the sacrifice of His body and blood on the cross, believers can experience a new birth, born of blood—not a natural birth, but a spiritual new creation made possible by His blood sacrifice.

Christian baptism became the sign that a believer had entered the new covenant. Paul discussed the theological application of baptism in Romans 6:4, when he wrote,

> *Therefore we were buried with Him through baptism into death, that just as Christ was raised from the dead by the glory of the Father, even so we also should walk in newness of life.*

Kingdom citizens enter the new realm by the new birth and receive a totally new life.

LAW OF LOVE

Every kingdom has laws that govern the conduct of its people. The Old Testament law was the code of Moses, delivered by God Himself at Mount Sinai. The New Testament law is quite different. Rather than being written on tablets of stone, it is engraved on *"tablets…of the heart"* (2 Corinthians 3:3).

Jesus expressed the tenets of kingdom law in His Sermon on the Mount, recorded in Matthew 5–7. He said that the spirit of the Old Testament law can be realized in a life guided by a desire to obey and please the heavenly Father:

> *Do not think that I came to destroy the Law or the Prophets. I did not come to destroy but to fulfill. For assuredly, I say to you, till heaven and earth pass away, one jot or one tittle will by no means pass from the law till all is fulfilled. Whoever therefore breaks one of the least of these commandments, and teaches men so, shall be called least in the kingdom of heaven; but whoever does and teaches them, he shall be called great in the kingdom of heaven.* (Matthew 5:17–19)

The blood of Jesus purchased a *"new and living way"* (Hebrews 10:20), a way of obedience to the law of love. That is the standard by which citizens live in the kingdom of God.

A DISTINCTIVE LIFESTYLE

Blood-bought kingdom citizens live such a different lifestyle from those around them that the world notices them and their distinctiveness. They live differently than they did before they came into the kingdom. Colossians 3:9–10 explains,

> *Do not lie to one another, since you have put off the old man with his deeds, and have put on the new man*

who is renewed in knowledge according to the image
of Him who created him.

Kingdom citizens make choices about how to conduct themselves based on what pleases God.

How can we make such a lifestyle a reality in our daily lives? Philippians 2:5 says, *"Let this mind be in you which was also in Christ Jesus."* The only way we can live by the law of love is to think as Jesus thought. This becomes possible when we are filled with the same Holy Spirit who indwells Him. *"For it is God who works in you both to will and to do for His good pleasure"* (Philippians 2:13).

THE ALREADY AND THE NOT YET

Some Bible teachers who discuss the expectations of those who lived before the coming of Christ use a compelling illustration to show how these people from earlier times perceived the impact of Messiah's coming and the initiation of the new kingdom. The teachers draw two circles side by side. The one on the left represents this present world. The one on the right represents the world to come. In between is a cataclysmic event: the coming of the Messiah Himself.

The perspective of people from ancient times was that the coming of the Messiah would initiate a completely new order of things. The old world ("this present world") would be done away with, and a new world ("the world to come") would replace it.

Those of us who live on this side of the New Testament understand that the drawing needs to be altered in order to be biblically correct. The two circles still represent this present world and the world to come; however, rather than being side by side, the two circles should overlap each other so that there is a space covered by both circles. It is in this space that the kingdom of God now exists. Kingdom citizens are still part of this present world, but they have also entered the world to come.

This is the nature of the blood-bought kingdom. On the one hand, the kingdom is a present, already realized reality. On the other hand, it is a kingdom of the future, not yet fully established.

Since Jesus died on the cross, paying the price for sin with His sacrificial blood, the enemy has been defeated. It was at Calvary that the kingdom came into being. It is a victorious kingdom, for Jesus Himself declared, *"I saw Satan fall like lightning from heaven"* (Luke 10:18). Satan's power is crushed, and his ultimate doom has already been decided.

While all this is true, we recognize that Satan has not admitted defeat. Although the sting has been taken from his power, the battle between good and evil will continue until the ultimate realization of the kingdom.

At the end of time and the beginning of eternity, the great hymn of glory will be the song of the blood and of praise to the Lamb who was slain. (See Revelation 5:12–14.) I believe that this song will usher in the fullness of the blood-bought kingdom of God. Until then, we can learn to live as kings and priests before our heavenly Father, living in the law of love and fulfilling His commands out of willing hearts.

13

THE POWER OF THE BLOOD TODAY

"Take heed to yourselves and to all the flock, among which the Holy Spirit has made you overseers, to shepherd the church of God which He purchased with His own blood."
—Acts 20:28

The blood of Jesus had—and has—the power to change history, and we are part of that history. Calvary is the focal point of the ages: All the ages before it looked forward to it, and all the ages since look back at it. There, against the skyline of the history of the world, is the cross of Christ with its message of eternal significance. Its essential message is this: Man is hopelessly lost without a Savior. Christ came to earth and died once and for all to bear sin's penalty on behalf on man and give him eternal life.

The symbol of atoning blood speaks clearly and loudly. Its clarion call echoes in every generation and reaches across the centuries. It is a call on our hearts and lives. First, how will we personally respond to the offer of eternal life through the sacrifice of the Lamb? Second, how will we live in response to this precious gift and its generous and loving Giver?

THE BLOOD HAS NEVER LOST ITS POWER

In the last chapter, we talked about the "already and not yet." We in the kingdom of God are in that place where the two circles overlap. We are in the kingdom, but we are also in the world. The covenant people of God, manifested in the church, are called to bring the message of redemption and deliverance through the blood to the hurting world in which we live. To this day, the blood has never lost its power. There is no limit to what Jesus's blood has accomplished and what it will accomplish as we live out our covenant relationship with God as His people—His church.

THE COVENANT PEOPLE OF GOD IN THE WORLD

The church is a precious creation of God. The blood-purchased people who belong to Him and do His work in the world have a specific mission entrusted to them.

WELCOMING THE PRESENCE OF GOD

The church can never accomplish the work of the Spirit by human ability alone. Its only hope is to seek and welcome the abiding presence of God. Describing the reality of this aspect of the church's mission, Ephesians 2:20–22 says,

> [You,] *having been built on the foundation of the apostles and prophets, Jesus Christ Himself being the chief corner stone, in whom the whole building, being joined together, grows into a holy temple in the Lord, in whom you also are being built together for a dwelling place of God in the Spirit.*

The highest calling of the called-out ones is to worship our God. He is worthy to be praised and extolled, His name lifted up as a testimony of His power and goodness. While the people of God in the Old Testament gathered to offer sacrifice, New Testament believers understand that the One Sacrifice has been offered, and they come together to

THE HIGHEST CALLING OF
THE CALLED-OUT ONES IS TO
WORSHIP OUR GOD. HE IS WORTHY
TO BE PRAISED AND EXTOLLED,
HIS NAME LIFTED UP AS A
TESTIMONY OF HIS POWER AND
GOODNESS. WHILE THE PEOPLE
OF GOD IN THE OLD TESTAMENT
GATHERED TO OFFER SACRIFICE,
NEW TESTAMENT BELIEVERS
UNDERSTAND THAT THE ONE
SACRIFICE HAS BEEN OFFERED,
AND THEY COME TOGETHER TO
CELEBRATE THE NAME OF THE
ONE WHO SHED HIS BLOOD FOR
OUR SALVATION.

celebrate the name of the One who shed His blood for our salvation.

The church, rightly functioning, is a place for God to dwell among His people.

PROCLAIMING THE MESSAGE OF CHRIST

As the covenant people of God, the church pleases God and ministers effectively in the world when it faithfully conveys the message that Christ has entrusted to it. This message is multifaceted and reflects both the words and example of Christ while He was here on earth.

Jesus cursed a fig tree because it failed to produce the fruit He expected of it. (See Matthew 21:19.) A church that fails to evangelize is like a fruitless tree that wastes the ground it is on or an abandoned house with *Ichabod* ("*the glory has departed*" 1 Samuel 4:21) written over its doors. Christ shed His precious blood that all men might be saved, but if the church does not tell men and women what He has done, it is fruitless.

It must break the heart of the Father to see a church doing everything else except what He has commissioned as its great work. We are God's redeemed people, and we have a responsibility to identify with and proclaim the truth of Jesus's great sacrifice. We must proclaim the one perfect Sacrifice who shed His blood to cleanse humanity of sin.

BRINGING GLORY TO GOD

One of the primary tasks of God's people is to bring Him glory. We do this by telling of God's revelation, recounting His mighty acts of power, and continually praising His name. Ephesians 3:20–21 counsels us to glorify Him in these words:

> Now to Him who is able to do exceedingly abundantly above all that we ask or think, according to the power that works in us, to Him be glory in the church by Christ Jesus to all generations, forever and ever. Amen.

MAKING KNOWN THE MANIFOLD WISDOM OF GOD

Man has always tried to figure out a way to arrange for his own salvation, but the judgment of God about man's attempts is succinctly expressed in 1 Corinthians 1:21:

> For since, in the wisdom of God, the world through wisdom did not know God, it pleased God through the foolishness of the message preached to save those who believe.

The world looks at the message of the gospel and declares it foolish. The idea of the blood of the Lamb having saving efficacy is thought to be insane by some. Yet the church itself is meant to be a manifestation of the wonderful wisdom of God demonstrated through the cross. Ephesians 3:10 says it this way: *"To the intent that now the manifold wisdom of God might be made known by the church to the principalities and powers in the heavenly places."* Paul knew that through the preaching of the gospel, that wisdom is revealed. *"I am not ashamed of the gospel of Christ, for it is the power of God to salvation for everyone who believes"* (Romans 1:16).

The good news of the gospel is that the blood avails for the redemption of the whole world and can be applied to any individual who hears the message and responds in repentance and love. The loving task of the church is to take the message of justification to all the world. *"By Him to reconcile all things to Himself, by Him, whether things on earth or things in heaven, having made peace through the blood of His cross"* (Colossians 1:20). We are called and commissioned to proclaim the good news and urge men and women to accept it.

The work of evangelism is generally fulfilled through preaching the Word, sharing personal testimony, sending missionaries, and utilizing media. Like Paul, we are to become all things to all men that by all means we might win some. (See 1 Corinthians 9:22.)

EDIFYING ITS MEMBERS

To edify means to build up, to grow. In its work of global outreach, the church must not neglect its own. The members of the body itself must not be overlooked or forgotten. They must be wrapped in loving fellowship and carefully nurtured by the Word for growth and Christian development. *"But if we walk in the light as He is in the light, we have fellowship one with another, and the blood of Jesus Christ His Son cleanses us from all sin"* (1 John 1:7).

I am more and more convinced, as I have become persuaded of the power of the blood to save, sanctify, and seal, that the great hope of the church to spread the message of the power of the blood is for God's people to be trained, prepared, and taught for this vital work.

As the church develops men and women to share the message of the gospel, at the same time the members themselves are growing in spiritual power and grace. This is God's plan for His blood-bought people.

When the church is faithfully putting forth the Word of God, something happens to its members: They grow up to become more and more like Christ:

And He Himself gave some to be apostles, some prophets, some evangelists, and some pastors and teachers, for the equipping of the saints for the work of ministry, for the edifying of the body of Christ, till we all come to the unity of the faith and of the knowledge of the

Son of God, to a perfect man, to the measure of the stature of the fullness of Christ. (Ephesians 4:11–13)

DISCIPLINING ITS MEMBERS

A passage in Revelation describes a church so displeasing to God that He says He will "spit it out of His mouth." (See Revelation 3:16 NIV.) God has a high expectation for His blood-bought sons and daughters. One of His expectations is that erring members will be corrected and disciplined. Jesus described the way in which this should be done:

> *Moreover if your brother sins against you, go and tell him his fault between you and him alone. If he hears you, you have gained your brother. But if he will not hear, take with you one or two more, that "by the mouth of two or three witnesses every word may be established." And if he refuses to hear them, tell it to the church. But if he refuses even to hear the church, let him be to you like a heathen and a tax collector.*
> (Matthew 18:15–17)

CARING FOR THOSE IN NEED

Jesus described the focus of His ministry using the passage in Isaiah that talks about visible, viable ministry to people. He inaugurated His public ministry by quoting Isaiah:

The Spirit of the LORD *is upon Me, because He has anointed Me to preach the gospel to the poor; He has sent Me to heal the brokenhearted, to proclaim liberty to the captives and recovery of sight to the blind, to set at liberty those who are oppressed; to proclaim the acceptable year of the* LORD.   (Luke 4:18–19)

His own ministry was marked by feeding the hungry, healing the sick, comforting the grieving, and causing the poor to rejoice. His called-out people can do no less. The Bible asks us,

If a brother or sister is naked and destitute of daily food, and one of you says to them, "Depart in peace, be warmed and filled," but you do not give them the things which are needed for the body, what does it profit? Thus also faith by itself, if it does not have works, is dead.   (James 2:15–17)

There is every expectation throughout the pages of the New Testament that God's people will be interested in taking care of the needs of the less fortunate. God's people are people of care. Our caring reflects the Spirit of the One of whom it is written,

How much more shall the blood of Christ, who through the eternal Spirit offered Himself without spot to God, cleanse your conscience from dead works to serve the living God? (Hebrews 9:14)

LIVING AS SANCTIFIED PEOPLE

Therefore Jesus also, that He might sanctify the people with His own blood, suffered outside the gate. Therefore let us go forth to Him, outside the camp, bearing His reproach. For here we have no continuing city, but we seek the one to come. Therefore by Him let us continually offer the sacrifice of praise to God, that is, the fruit of our lips, giving thanks to His name. But do not forget to do good and to share, for with such sacrifices God is well pleased.

(Hebrews 13:12–16)

Through the blood of Christ, we have been set apart and purchased for God. He has put His laws in our minds and written them on our hearts (see Hebrew 8:10), and we are to live as those who belong to Him and have His nature.

A significant way that we can remind ourselves often that we belong to God is through the celebration of the Lord's Supper, commemorating the shedding of Christ's blood on our behalf and the new life we receive through His sacrifice.

We remember the power of the blood every time we experience the Lord's Supper and share with fellow believers the

THROUGH THE BLOOD OF
CHRIST, WE HAVE BEEN SET
APART AND PURCHASED FOR GOD.
HE HAS PUT HIS LAWS IN OUR
MINDS AND WRITTEN THEM ON
OUR HEARTS (SEE HEBREW 8:10),
AND WE ARE TO LIVE AS THOSE
WHO BELONG TO HIM AND HAVE
HIS NATURE.

broken bread and the fruit of the vine. The power of the blood is brought close to home when we truly understand the significance of this sacrament.

At the institution of the Lord's Supper, Jesus expressed to His followers, *"But I say to you, I will not drink of this fruit of the vine from now on until that day when I drink it new with you in My Father's kingdom"* (Matthew 26:29). The church often doesn't grasp the true meaning of those words. We tend to place *"that day when I drink it new with you in My Father's kingdom"* into some far-off nebulous millennial future.

As a matter of fact, the kingdom became a reality for the disciples at the cross. The very next time they partook of the Supper, they were "drinking it new in the Father's kingdom." The happy message of this truth is that when we take part in the Lord's Supper, we have the assurance of His promise that He is present with us.

I challenge you to experience the Supper not as an empty ritual that is repeated "because we always do it," but rather see it as an occasion to actually enter the divine presence. Realize that He is at the table with you. He says to us today, as He did to those early disciples, *"With fervent desire I have desired to eat this Passover with you before I suffer"* (Luke 22:15).

With this understanding, the power of the blood will become a present reality to you. You will have the confidence to speak to Him as you share His meal. You will hear Him say something like, "It gives Me pleasure to fellowship with you. Is there anything you need? Is there anything I can help you with? What can I do to bless your life?"

When you approach the Sacrament in this intimate manner, realizing that He has desired to share this time with you, it will not be a historic symbol of a long-ago ritual but it will be a present-day manifestation of communion with God and the experience of His power—the power of the blood.

Therefore, when you go to communion, remember what God has done to wash your sins away, redeem you, heal you, and give you joy on this earth. Every blessing you enjoy is through the blood of the Lamb.

THE FUTURE OF THE CHURCH

I am overwhelmed with joy and pleasure when I think of the great love Christ has for the church and the glorious future He has prepared for it. Remember, it is the *"church of God which He purchased with His own blood"* (Acts 20:28). It is the church *"Christ…loved…and gave Himself for"* (Ephesians 5:25).

The prophet Malachi recorded these words of our heavenly Father:

"They shall be Mine," says the LORD *of hosts, "On the day that I make them My jewels. And I will spare*

them as a man spares his own son who serves him."
(Malachi 3:17)

The sons and daughters of the church have a present and future hope, and perhaps no one expressed it better than Titus:

> *For the grace of God that brings salvation has appeared to all men, teaching us that, denying ungodliness and worldly lusts, we should live soberly, righteously, and godly in the present age, looking for the blessed hope and glorious appearing of our great God and Savior Jesus Christ.*   (Titus 2:11–13)

Not only do we enjoy a high standard of holy living that pleases the Father in this present world, but we also have a blessed hope for the future. We're not sure of all the details of that future because much of its glories are hidden from our finite understanding. Some truths, however, are wonderfully clear and give us cause for rejoicing. For example, as John explained it,

> *Beloved, now we are children of God; and it has not yet been revealed what we shall be, but we know that when He is revealed, we shall be like Him, for we shall see Him as He is.*   (1 John 3:2)

Sons and daughters of the church should realize that this future day of rejoicing when we will see Him *"face to face"* (1 Corinthians 13:12) is also depicted in the book of Revelation and other passages that reveal the coming day of victory:

> *After these things I looked, and behold, a great multitude which no one could number, of all nations, tribes, peoples, and tongues, standing before the throne and before the Lamb, clothed with white robes, with palm branches in their hands, and crying out with a loud voice, saying, "Salvation belongs to our God who sits on the throne, and to the Lamb!"*
>
> (Revelation 7:9–10)

Then, at last, the Lamb of God will come into our clear view. The precious One whose blood was shed, the blood that made our salvation possible, will rejoice in the glory that is due Him. His people will gather before Him in a great paean of praise. All of heaven will resound with cries of praise and hallelujah.

The Lamb—He who was slain from the foundation of the world, He who was shamefully treated by heartless mobs, He whose sacrifice of blood was ignored by thoughtless millions—the One altogether lovely and worthy will at last be acknowledged by a grateful covenant people who will rejoice in His presence and look forward to eternity never separated from Him again.

TESTIMONIES OF THE POWER
OF THE BLOOD

A NAME WRITTEN IN HEAVEN

I was fourteen years of age when I was born again through the blood of our Lord Jesus Christ. A young pastor, the Reverend W. G. Abney, came to Warner Robins, Georgia, to plant a new church. He rented an old army barracks and began having services.

My mother and father began attending the services and were helping to establish the church. One Sunday night the Lord convicted me of my sins and I rushed to the altar to give my life to the Lord. The saints gathered around me to pray for my salvation.

I had been praying for only a short time when suddenly I found myself, in the Spirit, climbing a steep hill. It was very steep, and I began to pull at the bushes, trying to climb up the hill. Finally, I neared the top. As I did, I looked up and suddenly saw Jesus on the cross. His blood was dripping from His hands and feet. I pulled myself over until I was under the cross. I could literally feel the warm drops of Jesus's blood flowing over my soul.

I saw a huge book open up, and my name was written in large, golden letters in the book: THOMAS LANIER LOWERY.

I shall never forget the peace and ecstasy that flooded my soul that night. I knew my name was written in heaven. I knew God had a record of my commitment to Him as my soul was flooded with billows of joy beyond description. Such peace and happiness and fulfillment swept over me in waves of grandeur and blessing. What a happy day that was!

I have now served God for more than sixty years, and my love for Him increases with each passing year. I have never had a single desire to look back. He has kept me through the years—leading, guiding, protecting, providing for, and sustaining my family and me. I can truly say with David of old, *"I have not seen the righteous forsaken, nor his descendants begging bread"* (Psalm 37:25).

The rewarding ministry God has blessed me with has taken me around the world to preach the gospel in 115 different countries. Now, at age seventy-five, I am preparing for the next level in my ministry. I can hardly wait to see what God has in store for me!

—Dr. T. L. Lowery
International Evangelist
T. L. Lowery Global Ministries

THE BLOOD CLEANSES

As a young teenage boy of only fourteen, I accepted Jesus Christ as my Savior and realized the cleansing power of His blood. I came under deep conviction of my sins and my need for a Savior. Following a revival service one night, I could not sleep. I crawled out of my bed and began to repent of my sins. My father heard me praying and came in to pray with me.

My father had taught me that the blood of Jesus Christ, God's Son, cleanses from all sin. He assured me that confessed sins were under the blood. I rejoiced that night in the forgiveness of my sins, and I remain confident even now in the continuing, cleansing power of the precious blood of Jesus Christ.

—*James D. Leggett*
General Superintendent
International Pentecostal Holiness Church

MY TESTIMONY OF CONVERSION

I left home at age twelve and went to work on a farm. My life was taking me in a direction that was going far away from God. At that point in my life, I could not remember ever having heard anyone pray. At the age of fifteen, I was working in the fields of a cotton plantation in Mississippi County, Arkansas.

In the cotton field, I met a Church of God preacher who was, himself, picking cotton. A friendship developed between us, and he invited me to attend a meeting he was starting. I attended, and at first I stood outside and listened to the singing. Their music consisted of about a dozen different instruments; and boy, could those fellows play!

On the second night that I was there, a brother went to his car to get something and saw me standing in the shadows.

SOMETIMES WE GET
DISCOURAGED BECAUSE OUR
SLICK FORMULAS AND DOWN-PAT
CLICHES ARE NOT PRODUCING
BORN-AGAIN BELIEVERS; BUT
THEN THE POWER OF GOD WILL
FALL ON A SINCERE, REPENTANT
SINNER, AND WE DISCOVER IT
STILL WORKS LIKE IT HAS DOWN
THROUGH THE AGES.

He invited me inside. At first I made excuses, but he acted like he wanted me to come in, and I began to feel bad about refusing his invitation. So I went in, fully intending to leave as soon as the music and singing stopped.

When I was ready to leave, there were so many people between the door and me that I hated to disturb them by making them move. So I just waited and listened. Soon the minister asked everyone to stand while he gave the altar call for people to get saved.

I was suddenly aware that someone was standing beside me. When I glanced up, it was the preacher. He said to me, softly, "Son, wouldn't you like to get saved?" I had no idea what he was talking about, but he was treating me so kindly and courteously that I hated to say no. I just nodded my head yes.

"Come on, then," he said, and he led me like a child down to the altar. He said, "Just kneel down right there." Then he went back for others. I was at the altar but didn't know what to do. I didn't know a single word of prayer to say. Unexpectedly, I began to cry. I didn't know why I was crying, but I just felt like it.

About this time, two women came and knelt beside me and began to tell me things to say. One of them said to me, "Son, tell the Lord you want to be saved." I told Him. The other said, "Tell Him if He will save you, you will live for Him." I told Him that, too! In fact, everything they told me to say, I said. I began to mean it, and it happened that night—I was saved!

It was so wonderful; I felt so good. After a few minutes, I got up from the altar and walked over and stood against the wall, watching and listening. That was quite an experience hearing their praises and watching some of the people shout and dance. Some shouted, "Praise God!" Others said, "Hallelujah!" Still others cried out, "Glory to God!"

It sounded so good I thought I would like to try it. There was a lot of noise, so I thought that not many would hear me. I said, "Praise the Lord!" It felt so good I tried it again, this time louder. Before I hardly realized what I was doing, I was shouting loudly the praises to God that I had been hearing.

No one has been able to stop me since.

Sometimes we get discouraged because our slick formulas and down-pat cliches are not producing born-again believers; but then the power of God will fall on a sincere, repentant sinner, and we discover it still works like it has down through the ages.

I was one person when I walked down that little dirt road to the meeting that night but another person when I walked back to the place where I was staying. Jesus has now been my Savior and Lord for more than fifty-five years, and this experience gets sweeter as the days go by.

—*Rev. Paul H. Henson*
International Evangelist

HEALED BY THE BLOOD

THE NIGHT THE BLOOD BECAME REAL

I was saved through the bus ministry of a Nazarene church when I was eight years old. Because of a church split, I wound up in a Pilgrim Holiness church for a while. But when my backslidden mom and dad came back to the Lord, they wanted to attend a Pentecostal church because that was their background. We found the Church of God, and that is where we settled.

I was exposed to many Sunday School classes, youth programs, and lengthy sermons. However, by the time I was called to preach in my second year of Bible college, I was still woefully ignorant of some of the cardinal doctrines of the church. One of the teachings of the Scripture that particularly fascinated yet puzzled me was the concept of the blood of Christ.

In those days, we sang a lot of songs about the blood. "There Is Power in the Blood," "Nothing but the Blood," "Are You Washed in the Blood?" and "When I See the Blood" are some of them. I understood that the blood could cleanse and heal but had little knowledge about the power made possible through the sufferings of Christ. As a nineteen-year-old fledgling preacher, God was about to teach me a lesson I would never forget.

A TEST OF FAITH

During that second year of my Bible college training, I made jogging a regular part of my exercise routine. With no money to buy proper jogging footwear, I didn't realize how much I was endangering my feet as I ran on some rough, rocky trails with my thin tennis shoes. One day, on a quick run in the afternoon, I severely bruised my right heel on one of the trail stones. It was painful at the time, but I didn't think much about it because I had developed stone bruises before and they always cleared up in a couple of weeks with no complications.

This stone bruise was different. Instead of looking better after a few days and beginning to fade in color, it appeared to be growing in size and getting brighter in color. The pain was becoming more severe, at times making my whole foot throb. However, I was busy with classes and other school activities and didn't perceive the bruise to be anything serious. That perception began to change as the inflammation continued to spread until it covered all of my heel. The pain began to radiate up my leg to my knee. At night, the only way I could get relief from the intense throbbing was to elevate my leg with a pillow.

Had I been at home rather than in a college dormitory, I probably would have gone to the doctor before I did. When I finally called my mom and told her about the problem, she urged me to see a doctor immediately. She didn't have to convince me further; the pain had extended to my thigh.

The doctor's first words confirmed my greatest fear. "Son," he said, "you have waited too long." He went on to tell me it was his opinion that I had a type of cancer that had spread to my upper leg and was growing rapidly. Although he couldn't say for sure without more tests, he was concerned that the only way to stop the cancer and save my life was to amputate my right leg. Needless to say, that was a heavy message for a young man already making plans for marriage and excitedly looking forward to many years of successful ministry.

For some reason, however, I had a deep peace in my heart.

A MIRACLE OF HEALING

At the same time I received the diagnosis from the doctor, God's providence had Oral Roberts come to Fresno, California, where I was living, for a healing crusade. His huge ten-thousand-seat gospel tent had been set up at the county fairgrounds, and I knew what I had to do. Without hesitation, I secured a prayer card, and on the third night, I found myself standing in a long line across the front, waiting for my time with the great healing evangelist.

When I stood before Oral Roberts and handed him my prayer card, I felt very insignificant and frightened to be the focus of attention. He paused a moment as he read the information on my card.

"So you're a young preacher and you have cancer. Is that right?"

"Yes, sir."

"Do you believe God is going to heal you tonight?"

"Yes, sir."

He laid his hand on my head and prayed a short prayer. I didn't feel anything spiritual. Then he asked me to take off my shoe and stomp my right foot. As I removed my shoe, I looked down at the corrugated aluminum platform with its raised metal cleats. I knew I was in trouble. When my throbbing foot hit the metal platform, the pain was so excruciating I thought I would fly through the roof of the tent. He saw the pain on my face.

"That hurt, didn't it?"

"Yes, sir."

Then with obvious determination and compassion, he said, "We're going to pray again." When the man of God prayed the second time, immediately I felt a bolt of supernatural power surge through my body. It began at the top of my head and flowed out through my right foot. Without hesitation, I began to stomp my foot again. This time, the more I stomped it, the better it felt. I kept stomping. I stomped both feet. It was a feeling like I had never experienced.

When I realized where I was, it seemed that all ten thousand people in the tent were on their feet, shouting and praising God for the evident miracle they had just witnessed. There was no doubt in my mind; I knew God had supernaturally intervened in my life and rebuked the cancer in my body. The blood of Jesus Christ had cleansed my physical system of the cancerous cells. By His stripes I was healed!

WHEN THE BLOOD BECAME REAL

For the rest of that night, I was on a spiritual high. I was interviewed by a reporter from the local newspaper, and I felt a powerful anointing as I answered her questions. An overwhelming joy flowed out of me to every person I spoke with. It was quite an evening, and when I finally got to my room, I was ready to lie down on my bed and drift off to sleep. I continued to bask in the glory of God.

The moment I hit the bed, however, I knew something was wrong. As I stretched out my right leg, a sharp pain shot up into my thigh. The throbbing began again with a vengeance. Instinctively, I jumped out of bed and fell to my knees. I felt a spiritual authority well up inside of me.

"Satan, you are not going to put this cancer back on me. The blood of Jesus Christ is against you! You are defeated! The blood of Jesus prevails!" The Holy Spirit took control of my tongue and began to rebuke the devil in another language. I didn't understand the words, but I knew exactly what the Spirit was saying.

After about thirty minutes, I got back into bed and immediately fell asleep. When I awoke in the morning, I was thoroughly refreshed and there was no pain whatsoever. Two weeks later the cancer in my heel dried up and fell out. The cavity it left soon closed over and left no trace of the evil that had threatened my life. To this day there has never been any indication of a recurrence of the cancer.

That night in my bedroom, as I battled the devil for control of my life and future, I learned once and for all the reality and power of the blood of Jesus. I have never been the same.

> What can wash away my sin?
> Nothing but the blood of Jesus;
> What can make me whole again?
> Nothing but the blood of Jesus.[1]

—Robert E. Fisher, Ph.D.
Executive Director
Center for Spiritual Renewal

KEPT BY THE BLOOD

WHEN SATAN OPPRESSES

Roy Tucker, a very great pastor, described to me an encounter he had with demonic powers. It was a bizarre and terrifying experience that shows the ferocity and intensity of battling the forces of evil in spiritual warfare.

He said he first thought he was having a dream. He could feel something—it felt like a physical presence—pressing on his body. He felt weighted down, paralyzed. He could not imagine what was happening to him. He said it was as though he was screaming, but not a sound was coming out of his mouth. Roy knew an enemy from Satan had come to do something terrible to him. He knew in his spirit that this was a spiritual attack from the devil himself.

It was the middle of the night when he awoke; it was pitch dark. He could hear voices, as if someone was in the room with him, so he tried to open his eyes, but He could not. In fact, he could not move any part of his body. He tried to call out to someone for help but could not make a sound. He could not even move his lips.

The voices grew louder and louder. Soon they were close to him—right up next to him—screaming in his ears. He knew the voices belonged to evil spirits. With wild, raucous voices, they were scolding him for something he had or had not done—something that had offended them.

Then, he said, he felt his body floating upward; he was levitating from the bed. He found himself hovering against the ceiling, unable to move or speak or do anything. The screaming voices continued their relentless assault on his senses. He thought he was going mad. He actually thought he was going to die!

Gradually, his eyes opened and he could look around, but he could not do anything else. In addition to the voices, He sensed a malevolent presence in the room with him. Because of the pressure on his chest, he had difficulty breathing. As the evil spirit tormented him, he experienced sheer terror.

Finally, he had the presence of mind to realize that he could fight against this extreme spiritual attack of the devil. He willed himself to cry out, in his mind, "In the name of Jesus, and in the power of the blood of the Lamb, I resist the devil and all his evil spirits." Immediately, he felt a lessening of the pressure!

Complete deliverance did not come immediately. But as he kept repeating the name of Jesus and calling on the blood of the Lamb, he became more free and more able to move and speak. By now, he could whisper, "Jesus, Jesus." His voice grew louder and stronger, and he was liberated from the oppressive power of the enemy by the precious blood of Jesus Christ. Satan, the blood of Jesus is against you!

THE TRANSCENDENT LIFE OF AGAPE LOVE

Thanksgiving Day 1980 was family day at Grandmother's house in Tennessee. It was a day of laughter, songs, play, and general fellowship with uncles, aunts, cousins, and extended families all coming together to form one great family. It was one of those perfect days of family interaction and reunion.

Little did we know that just thirty-six hours later a tragic phone call would come, informing us that our son, Paul Dana, and his wife, Julie, had been involved in a head-on automobile collision on the way home from the celebration.

Early in the morning in a motel room in Tennessee, I picked up the phone and heard an unknown voice from a faceless doctor say, "Your son and his wife have had an accident. Julie is seriously injured, but she will recover. Your son was killed instantly. Where do you want us to send his body?"

Only those who have experienced this shock can understand the dull ache and fear that accompany such a tragedy. In one terrible moment, the joyous closeness of Thanksgiving changed to the empty loss of death. The joy of having a first-born son who fulfilled every expectation—he was an athlete, musician, and pastor—and brought nothing but pleasure and pride was changed to numbness. *This can't possibly be true! Somebody tell us that this is all a big mistake!*

What do we do when tragedy strikes? We hurt. We hurt when we have to confront the tragedy of divorce. We hurt when we have to face the tragedy that our children have become drug addicts. We hurt when we deal with the tragedy of bankruptcy. We hurt when we get the tragic news that the tumor is malignant and the prognosis is not good. We hurt when we experience the finality of a loved one's death.

But we also do something else: We turn to the deepest resources within us and draw on the rudiments of our faith to sustain us. We engage in spiritual warfare and realize that

God is calling us to live the transcendent life. This is the essential meaning of faith—to become a transcender, to go beyond the limits, to step over the boundaries, to surpass the limiting factors, to rise above the hindrances, to cope with the uncontrollable, and to know that, regardless of the circumstances, *"we are more than conquerors through Him who loved us"* (Romans 8:37).

In the loss of our son, my wife, Carmelita, and I learned trust in the Word of the Lord, which makes it clear that God has given us *"exceedingly great and precious promises, that through these [we] may be partakers of the divine nature, having escaped the corruption that is in the world through lust"* (2 Peter 1:4).

What are these precious promises? How may we be heirs of God and joint heirs with Christ? How do we "fight the fight" in the face of death?

First, we can expect God to work for good in all things. This is the universal promise of Romans 8:28. Everything that happens to us is not necessarily "good" within itself. It often hurts. Yet we know that the long-term effects of every situation blend together for a symphony of eternal good under the direction of the Father.

Second, we can expect God to finish what He has begun in our lives. This is the promise of Philippians 1:6: *"Being confident of this very thing, that He who has begun a good work in you will complete it until the day of Jesus Christ.*" One translator says, "He will put His finishing touches on you." It doesn't really matter how small or how large our faith may be. In God's mind, the plan formulated is just as good as the plan accomplished. We will someday be glorified because God completes every good work that He begins. (See Philippians 3:21.) This means that the ultimate goal in spiritual warfare is to live the transcendent life—regardless!

Third, expect the Spirit to make intercession when you are having problems. Paul exclaimed in Romans 8:31, "*If God is for us, who can be against us?*" God affirms, and He also acts on our behalf. He actually promises to give us victory in the midst of crisis. Paul declared in Romans 8:37, "*Yet in all these things we are more than conquers through Him who loved us.*" Inside ourselves we have the capacity to overcome, even though we have to be resigned to the fallout of a frustrated creation, the limitations of human weakness, the sting of death, and the continuing problem of evil promoted by a secularized worldview.

Fourth, we can expect God to keep us in His love. The Scriptures say,

> *Who shall separate us from the love of Christ? Shall tribulation, or distress, or persecution, or famine, or nakedness, or peril, or sword?…I am persuaded that neither death nor life, nor angels nor principalities nor powers, nor things present nor things to come, nor*

> *height nor depth, nor any other created thing, shall be able to separate us from the love of God which is in Christ Jesus our Lord.* (Romans 8:35, 38–39)

This means that one of the great weapons given to us for spiritual warfare is agape love. In this regard, the only way we can learn agape love is to live the transcendent life. Agape love is the giving of self. This law of love is the supreme law of eternity. The problem is that this love has to be learned within the confines of time. Only upon this earth and in this environment can this transcendent triumph of God's love be molded in such a way that we will be qualified to administer the law of love in eternity. Billheimer makes the point that natural affection does not have to be learned. Agape love is only learned by being utterly broken, by suffering without resentment.

Once we learn this lesson of the transcendent life, the very meaning of 2 Corinthians 1:3–4 comes alive in a new and literal way:

> *Blessed be the God and Father of our Lord Jesus Christ, the Father of mercies and God of all comfort, who comforts us in all our tribulation, that we may be able to comfort those who are in any trouble, with the comfort with which we ourselves are comforted by God.*

Perhaps the transcendent life of agape love is best described in the following letter that I received from Pat Robertson, Founder and Chairman of CBN, at the time of our son's death:

Dear Paul,

I wanted you to know that I have been praying for you and your wife in your time of grief. I know that you will be surrounded by the love of thousands at this time but if there is any way that I can personally assist you other than in prayer please let me know. God must have something very special for you in the years ahead. When I thought of you, the words of the apostle Peter came to mind.

"In this you greatly rejoice, even though now for a little while, if necessary, you have been distressed by various trials, that the proof of your faith, being more precious than gold which is perishable, even though tested by fire, may be found to result in praise and glory and honor at the revelation of Jesus Christ" (1 Peter 1:6–7 NASB).

We are not immune from tragedy. The good news, however, is that we can transcend our tragedies. We know that God is a God of miracles (see Hebrews 11:1–35), but God is also a God of maintenance faith (see Hebrews 11:36–40).

As Hebrews 11:40 states, the transcendent life of agape love means that God has planned something better for us so that only together with us would both miracle and maintenance be made perfect.

—*Paul L. Walker, Ph.D.*
Assistant General Overseer
Church of God International

NOTES

CHAPTER TWO

1. M. R. DeHaan, M.D., *The Chemistry of the Blood* (Grand Rapids, Michigan: Zondervan Publishing House, 1943, 1981), 14.

2. http://www.bloodcenters.org/aboutblood/bloodfacts.htm.

3. Ibid.

4. http://www.redcross.org/prepare/giveblood.html.

5. H. A. Maxwell Whyte, *The Power of the Blood* (New Kensington: Whitaker House, 1973), 17.

6. M. R. DeHaan, *The Chemistry of the Blood*, 25 (author's emphasis).

CHAPTER THREE

1. Merrill C. Tenney, ed., *The Zondervan Pictorial Bible Dictionary* (Grand Rapids, Michigan: Regency Reference Library from Zondervan Publishing House, 1967), 739–40.

2. Merrill F. Unger, *The New Unger's Bible Dictionary*, R. K. Harrison, Ed. (Chicago: Moody Press, 1988), 1102.

3. Ibid.

4. Ibid., 1104.

5. *The Zondervan Pictorial Bible Dictionary*, 740.

6. Merrill F. Unger, *The New Unger's Bible Dictionary*, 1106.

7. Ibid., 1107.

8. See *NASC* #H3725 and #H3724a. All footnotes marked (*NASC*) are from the *New American Standard Exhaustive Concordance of the Bible*, © 1981 by The Lockman Foundation. All rights reserved.

9. See *NASC*, #H5799.

CHAPTER FOUR

1. For a discussion of the medical aspects of scourging and crucifixion, please refer to David Terasaka, M.D., "Medical Aspects of the Crucifixion of Jesus Christ" at http://www.new-life.net/crucify1.htm> and <http://www.new-life.net/crucify2.htm.

2. http://www.tscpulpitseries.org/english/1990s/ts960415.html.

3. Elvina M. Hall, "I Hear the Savior Say," 1865.

CHAPTER FIVE

1. William Walford, "Sweet Hour of Prayer," 1845.

CHAPTER SEVEN

1. http://www.interhack.net/projects/library/vine/T0002350.html#T0002356.

2. Robert Lowry, "What Can Wash Away My Sin?" 1876.

3. William Cowper, "There Is a Fountain Filled with Blood," 1771.

CHAPTER NINE

1. Merrill F. Unger, *The New Unger's Bible Dictionary*, R. K. Harrison, Ed. (Chicago: Moody Press, 1988), 1102.

CHAPTER ELEVEN

1. St. Catherine of Siena, *The Dialogue of St. Catherine of Siena*, trans. Algar Thorold (Rockford, Illinois: TAN Books and Publishers, 1991).

TESTIMONIES OF THE POWER OF
THE BLOOD

1. Robert Lowry, "What Can Wash Away My Sin?" 1876.

ABOUT THE AUTHOR

Mary K. Baxter was born in Chattanooga, Tennessee. While she was a girl, her mother taught her about Jesus Christ and His salvation. Although she felt called by God at that time, she was truly born again when she was a young woman and God revealed Himself to her as Savior at the same time He miraculously healed her newborn child.

In 1976, while she was living in Belleville, Michigan, Jesus appeared to her in human form, in dreams, visions, and revelations. During those visits, He revealed to her the depths, degrees, levels, and torments of lost souls in hell, telling her that this message is for the whole world. Since that time, she has received many visitations from the Lord. In God's wisdom, to give balance to her message, she has also received many visions, dreams, and revelations of heaven, angels, and the end of time.

On Mary's tours of hell, she walked with Jesus and talked with many people. Jesus showed her what happens to unrepentant souls when they die and what happens to servants of God when they do not remain obedient to their calling, go back into a life of sin, and refuse to repent.

Mary was ordained as a minister in 1983 at a Full Gospel church in Taylor, Michigan, and recently received a Doctor of Ministry degree from Faith Bible College, Independence, Missouri. Ministers, leaders, and saints of the Lord around the world speak very highly of her and her ministry. The movement of the Holy Spirit is emphasized in all her services, and many miracles have occurred in them. The gifts of the Holy Spirit with demonstrations of power are manifested in her meetings as the Spirit of God leads and empowers her.

Mary, a mother and grandmother, loves the Lord with everything she has—all her heart, mind, soul, and strength. She is truly a dedicated handmaiden of the Lord, and she desires above all to be a soulwinner for Jesus Christ. From the headquarters of Divine Revelation, Inc., her Florida-based ministry, this anointed evangelist continues to travel the world, speaking at conferences, seminars, and other gatherings and telling her story of heaven and hell and her revelatory visits from the Lord.

Gen 6-5-6   God Regetted man was

Hebrew Word the atonement is
"Kaphar", To cover,

K ^{Yom}ippur Hebrew for, the Price of Life
   Lev 16

~~Jesus~~ Layed his own Life down willing
John 10:17-18 To Reckon on Human Race to ~~25~~
See Temple Vail Ripe

I Peter 1- 18_

Welcome to Our House!

We Have a Special Gift for You

It is our privilege and pleasure to share in your love of Christian books. We are committed to bringing you authors and books that feed, challenge, and enrich your faith.

To show our appreciation, we invite you to sign up to receive a specially selected **Reader Appreciation Gift**, with our compliments. Just go to the Web address at the bottom of this page.

God bless you as you seek a deeper walk with Him!

WE HAVE A GIFT FOR YOU. VISIT:

whpub.me/nonfictionthx

WHITAKER
HOUSE